Employment Tribunals

Employment Tribunals

Their Growth and the Case for Radical Reform

J. R. SHACKLETON

The Institute of Economic Affairs

First published in Great Britain in 2002 by
The Institute of Economic Affairs
2 Lord North Street
Westminster
London SW1P 3LB
in association with Profile Books Ltd

A CIP catalogue record for this book is available from the British Library.

ISBN 0 255 36515 2 ✓

Many IEA publications are translated into languages other than English or
are reprinted. Permission to translate or to reprint should be sought from the
General Director at the address above.

Typeset in Stone by MacGuru
info@macguru.org.uk

Printed and bound in Great Britain by Hobbs the Printers

CONTENTS

Author's note   7
The author   8
Foreword   9
Summary   11
List of tables and figures   13

1   Introduction   15

2   What do tribunals do?   21
    Types of application   24
    How tribunals work   26
    Compensation   32

3   The rise of the tribunals   35
    No freedom of contract   35
    Goodbye to Kahn-Freund   40
    Individual rather than collective rights   45
    Unions and tribunals   47
    The rest of Europe   49
    The economics of uncertainty and the rise of tribunal
        applications   52

4 The costs of the tribunal system   61
   Direct resource costs   61
   Compensation   64
   Compliance costs   65
   Indirect costs   67
   Emphasis on costs misleads   68

5 The wider costs of labour market regulation   70
   Labour market regulation as a 'stealth tax'   70
   The distributional impact   73

6 Who applies to tribunals?   81
   Discrimination applications   83
   Unfair dismissal applications   86

7 Reforming the tribunal system   90
   Tribunal ownership   90
   Alternative dispute resolution   92
   DTI proposals and the Employment Bill   96
   Do we need tribunals in their current form?   100
   Other ways of regulating   103
   The commissions   105
   A return to voluntarism?   108

8 Conclusions   113

   About the IEA   116

AUTHOR'S NOTE

Since completion of this Hobart Paper in early July 2002, the Employment Bill has completed its journey through Parliament and become the Employment Act 2002. The Employment Tribunal System Taskforce has reported, making a number of minor procedural and practical recommendations. Its report can be accessed at http://www.employmenttribunalsystemtaskforce. gov.uk. Provisional figures for tribunal applications in 2001–02 show a slight fall from the peak of 2000–01. However the Taskforce points out that the fall was mainly in multiple applications (where a test case can resolve many applications) and suggests that the long-term trend is for the Employment Tribunals Service caseload to continue to increase.

A great many people have helped me in preparing this paper and by commenting on a draft. They include Cecilie Bingham, Michael Connolly, John Crosby, Professor David Henderson, Geoffrey Killick, Professor David Lewis, Elisabeth Michielsens, Christine Porter, David Rees, Professor Colin Robinson, Professor Stanley Siebert, Tony Swabe, Peter Urwin and the anonymous IEA referees. I have benefited considerably from all their advice, notwithstanding its occasional inevitable contradictions.

THE AUTHOR

J. R. Shackleton is Professor of Economics at the University of Westminster and Head of Westminster Business School. He was educated at King's College, Cambridge, and the School of Oriental and African Studies, University of London. He has taught at a number of universities and has worked as an economic adviser in the Government Economic Service.

Professor Shackleton has lectured to audiences in several countries and has appeared frequently on radio and TV. He has published extensively, mainly in the field of labour economics. Recent books include (with Thomas Lange, editor) *The Political Economy of German Unification* (Berghahn, 1998) and *Training for Employment in Western Europe and the United States* (Edward Elgar, 1995). He is a member of the IEA's Academic Advisory Council, and has published for the Institute *Training Too Much?* (Hobart Paper 118) and *Trouble in Store?* (with Terry Burke, Hobart Paper 130).

FOREWORD

Employment tribunals are now a well-established feature of the British economy. They began life in the 1960s as industrial tribunals with the principal task of hearing employer appeals against training levies, but, as Professor Shackleton explains in Hobart Paper 145, in the intervening years their scope has greatly expanded. They now have jurisdiction over more than eighty types of complaint, including unfair dismissal, discrimination on grounds of race, sex and disability, breach of contract and unlawful deductions.

The tribunal system has become very costly, when both direct and indirect costs are taken into account, and is the source of many complaints from employers. The total costs, though difficult to quantify, appear in the form of uncertainty, stress at work, erosion of trust, increases in business costs and – most important in Professor Shackleton's view – discouragement of job creation. Indeed, he argues that the labour market regulation which the tribunals enforce is a type of 'stealth tax' on employment which, contrary to popular belief, does not only affect employers. Employees 'pay in terms of lower wages and reduced job opportunities'. Furthermore, the costs fall unequally on different groups of workers and potential workers.

What can be done about this costly imposition on the British labour market? Professor Shackleton is not hopeful about the government's efforts to promote procedural changes intended to reduce tribunal applications, particularly since there is a 'seemingly inexhaustible drive for further labour market regulation from the European Union'. To make progress, he argues in his final two chapters, there should be a halt to further regulation and a move towards greater freedom of contract in the labour market. Employers and employees would, by and large, be left to contract freely without the burden of the present mass of government rules. There seems little enthusiasm in Britain at present for such a move, and still less enthusiasm in the other EU countries. However, argues Professor Shackleton, a change of mood might occur if there was a recession in Europe. That would 'remind people forcefully that employers who create jobs are more likely to be public benefactors in the long run than those who seek to restrict ever more narrowly the conditions under which employment contracts can be formed' (p. 115).

As in all Institute publications, the views expressed in Hobart Paper 145 are those of the author, not those of the Institute (which has no corporate view), its managing trustees, Academic Advisory Council members or senior staff. Professor Shackleton's analysis of and challenge to the employment tribunal system is published as a significant contribution to public debate about one of the most contentious features of British business life.

COLIN ROBINSON

Editorial Director, Institute of Economic Affairs

Professor of Economics, University of Surrey

August 2002

SUMMARY

- Applications to employment tribunals have nearly trebled in the last decade and are now running at well over 100,000 a year.
- There are now over eighty different 'jurisdictions' covering such matters as unfair dismissal, breach of contract, race, sex and disability discrimination, parental leave and working time. On average each application covers 1.7 jurisdictions.
- The decline of trade unionism from the late 1970s saw a movement away from 'collective' to 'individual' rights, accentuated by changes in the composition of the workforce and legislation both from the UK and European Union directives.
- One major problem is the continuing level of uncertainty as a result of frequent changes in the law and its interpretation. This leads to speculative applications and inadvertent breaches of the law by employers.
- The tribunal system imposes substantial direct and indirect costs on taxpayers, and on businesses and individuals involved with applications. Nevertheless, the really significant impact of labour market regulation of whatever form is 'stealth taxation' on employment, which impacts on the economy as a whole. The burden falls unequally on different groups of employees and potential employees.

- Analysis of tribunal applications suggests that some individuals are better placed to use tribunals than others, and that this form of enforcement of labour market regulation may not be well targeted.
- Large firms and public sector and voluntary organisations are disproportionately likely to face discrimination claims, despite being more likely to have explicit equal opportunities policies.
- Current government reforms to employment tribunal procedures are unlikely to have a major impact.
- Other possible reforms include altering the structure of tribunals, substituting an inspectorate to enforce some types of regulation, the use of the tax and benefit system rather than employer mandates, and reducing the influence of the Equal Opportunities Commission, the Commission for Racial Equality and the Disability Rights Commission.
- Significant reductions in tribunal applications are, however, likely to require substantial deregulation in the labour market and a move towards greater freedom of contract.

TABLES AND FIGURES

Table 1   The growth of tribunal powers – main relevant
            legislation and regulations   22
Table 2   Categories of application as percentage of total   25
Table 3   Outcome of tribunal applications 2000/01   28
Table 4   Compensation awarded by employment tribunals,
            2000/01   33
Table 5   Union criteria for supporting claims   48
Table 6   Some estimates of the resource costs of the tribunal
            system, 2000/01   62
Table 7   Indirect costs incurred by employers in
            tribunal cases   67
Table 8   Tribunal applications by size of workplace   82
Table 9   Employment tribunals and ACAS arbitration: a
            comparison   94
Table 10   The DTI proposals   98

Figure 1   Registered tribunal applications, Great Britain   24
Figure 2   Stoppages and working days lost per thousand
            employees, UK, 1980–2001   44
Figure 3   Impact of a mandated worker benefit   71

1   INTRODUCTION

Employment tribunals are rarely out of the news, and they generally get a bad press. A search of newspaper websites will always throw up a rich crop of apparently weird and wacky cases. Here are just a few recent examples:

- A jobcentre manager is awarded thousands of pounds compensation, claiming that racism on the part of her employers has damaged her promotion prospects despite the fact that she has turned down four offers of a more senior job. She is then promoted to a job she likes, but within a year she successfully takes the Employment Service before a tribunal again, claiming that fellow workers have gossiped about her and victimised her (*Mail on Sunday*, 26 August 2001).
- A harassed hotel owner, faced with large numbers of guests coming down to breakfast at once, shouts for an extra teapot. Taking offence at the abrupt nature of the request, an employee walks out and takes him to a tribunal, claiming constructive (unfair) dismissal. The hotel pays over £10,000 to settle the action and avoid a full hearing (*Sunday Times*, 17 June 2001).
- The Law Society runs up costs of £1 million defending itself against claims of race and sex discrimination made by its former vice-president, who has previously been forced to

resign after allegations that she bullied and harassed staff. Despite finding that the complainant has indeed created an atmosphere of 'fear and dread', and also lied under oath, a tribunal finds in her favour after a six-week hearing (*Financial Times*, 26 July 2001).

- An employee is caught dealing in cannabis at work and admits he has been doing so for some time. He is dismissed, but claims unfair dismissal and his notice money. The case goes to a hearing, but he does not turn up. Nevertheless, the company's representatives have to go through the evidence to get the case rejected (*Daily Telegraph*, 10 September 2001).
- An accountant makes an application to a tribunal under the Disability Discrimination Act. Her disability is described as 'acute anxiety about her work performance', which prevents her working to deadlines or submitting herself to appraisal; she argues that the employer has not sufficiently adjusted her working conditions to take account of this. At lunch-time during the tribunal hearing, she disappears and the tribunal abandons the case. The employer is left with substantial, irrecoverable legal costs (*Guardian*, 1 November 2000).
- A 35-year-old City analyst earning a basic £120,000 a year is awarded a 'lousy' annual bonus of only £25,000. She resigns her post and claims constructive dismissal and sex discrimination. After a four-day hearing a tribunal awards her £1.4 million compensation (*Guardian*, 11 January 2002).

With cases like these, an outraged 'what is the world coming to?' response is common, particularly among those of an older generation brought up on a rhetoric of duties rather than rights. However, each outcome is defensible in terms of existing legislation and, one supposes, in terms of the subjective hurt experienced by the complainants. Moreover, if these examples appear to cast tribunal applicants in a bad light, it is equally possible to recount a string of stories illustrating generally unacceptable employer behaviour such as gross sexual misconduct or cheating employees out of pay they are owed. So we should not rush to judgement. We need to leave the anecdotal approach to one side, and look at the employment tribunal system more systematically and analytically.

There is certainly a real issue to think about, for applications to employment tribunals have risen dramatically. In the last ten years they have nearly trebled and are currently running at well over 100,000 per year. The pressure on the Employment Tribunals Service (ETS) is growing. In 1998/99 one of the ETS's targets was getting 85 per cent of simple cases to a tribunal within 26 weeks; it achieved 89 per cent. In 2000/01, against the same target, it was only able to achieve 77 per cent.[1]

Is this explosion of tribunal activity indicative of something going fundamentally wrong in the workplace, with employees suffering from an increasingly harsh and uncaring management culture? Or is it, rather, evidence of the malign effects of growing labour market regulation, generating a 'compensation culture' and imposing costs that far outweigh considerations of public utility, and ultimately threaten jobs?

Interest groups have taken opposed positions on the issue. On the one hand union leaders argue that 'in many cases, employment tribunals are the only recourse some people have to workplace jus-

---

1   Employment Tribunals Service Annual Reports.

tice'.[2] They see the workplace as characterised by inequality, with employers often abusing their power to deprive workers of a fair deal. John Monks of the TUC claims that, although 'unions would prefer the number of tribunal claims to go down ... the situation won't change until bad bosses start treating their staff fairly'.[3]

Unsurprisingly, employers' organisations don't see 'bad bosses' as the main problem. The Engineering Employers' Federation claims that 'the avalanche of employment legislation ... has fuelled an ever-increasing culture of litigation. Employers are now facing the problem of defending more and more cases at a time when their companies are already under pressure.'[4] Richard Wilson, Business Policy Executive at the Institute of Directors (IOD), argues that the result of the growing role of tribunals 'will inevitably be further costs on business ... the impact on small enterprises could be particularly serious'.[5] Digby Jones of the Confederation of British Industry (CBI) argues that 'in too many cases the tribunal system is the solution of first resort rather than last resort ... while most cases are genuine, firms are worried that a punt-for-cash culture is taking hold'.[6] The Director-General of the British Chambers of Commerce laments that 'the burden of proof now almost rests on the employer to prove that they didn't do something wrong ... in that sort of situation, most firms' lawyers would advise them to settle out of court even if ... they haven't done anything wrong'.[7]

He has some grounds for this particular assertion. The De-

---

2   Tony Burke of the Graphical, Paper and Media Union, quoted in the *Observer*, 5 August 2001.

3   Quoted on Ananova website, 25 July 2001.

4   Engineering Employers' Federation press release, 1 March 2001.

5   IOD press release, 12 February 1999.

6   CBI press release, 21 August 2001.

7   BBC Business News website, 7 February 2001.

partment of Trade and Industry (DTI) reports that 43 per cent of employers who settle out of court do so despite thinking that a tribunal would have rejected the applicant's case.[8] Digby Jones says that this 'seems like a 21st century version of Danegeld', with tribunal applicants cast as the marauding Danes.

The government has shown its own concern about the growth of tribunal applications. In the summer of 2001 the DTI issued a consultation paper, *Routes to Resolution: Improving Dispute Resolution in Britain*, proposing a number of reforms and inviting suggestions. Following a period of consultation, some of these proposals were incorporated into the new Employment Bill, while an Employment Tribunals System Taskforce was set up to consider administrative reforms to the system. In a related development, the Advisory Conciliation and Arbitration Service (ACAS)[9] recently announced a scheme for the resolution of unfair dismissal cases which is meant to reduce the need for recourse to full tribunal hearings.

Change is thus in the air. This is a timely moment to take stock of the history and development of employment tribunals, and to look more closely at the economic impact of these institutions. One commentator has observed that 'no comprehensive evaluation of the costs and benefits of the employment tribunal system

---

8   Department of Trade and Industry, *Routes to Resolution: Improving Dispute Resolution in Britain*, July 2001.

9   The Advisory Conciliation and Arbitration Service is an independent (though publicly funded) body which has a statutory duty to conciliate in most employment tribunal jurisdictions where applicants and respondents are willing to consider conciliation. It was set up in the 1970s primarily to assist in the conciliation of collective industrial disputes, but settling individual employees' complaints is now by far the biggest area of ACAS's work. Its budget in 2000/01 was just over £33 million.

has ever been undertaken'.[10] He is right. This Hobart Paper may not be that comprehensive evaluation, but the intention is to make a stab at this difficult task.

---

10   M. Emmott, 'Tribunals are judged wanting', *Guardian*, 12 March 2001.

2 WHAT DO TRIBUNALS DO?

We begin by examining the nature of the beast. Employment tribunals are the main official means of resolving disputes relating to individual employment rights in this country. Oddly, they were not originally set up for this purpose at all. They started life in the mid-1960s as industrial tribunals, the name by which they continued to be officially known until the 1998 Employment Rights (Dispute Resolutions) Act. Their main original purpose was to hear employer appeals against training levies imposed by the Industrial Training Act of 1964. However, their responsibilities were extended to hearing individual employees' cases under the Redundancy Payments Act of 1965. This was followed by a major expansion of jurisdiction with the 1968 Race Relations Act, the introduction of equal pay legislation in 1970, and protection against unfair dismissal in the Industrial Relations Act of 1971. The Sex Discrimination Act of 1975 was another major landmark in the development of tribunal powers.

In the last 25 years or so the scope of tribunal competence in these areas has been greatly enhanced by legal judgments, amending legislation and EU directives. This happened even during the long period of Conservative administrations. Some new jurisdictions, for example in relation to trade unions and Sunday working, were added as by-products of Tory reforms in the 1980s and 1990s, and in 1995 the Disability Discrimination Act led to a further

Table 1 **The growth of tribunal powers – main relevant legislation and regulations**

Date	Legislation	Comment
1964	Industrial Training Act	Established tribunals
1965	Redundancy Payments Act	Tribunals available to employees
1968	Race Relations Act	
1970	Equal Pay Act	
1971	Industrial Relations Act	Created concept of unfair dismissal
1974	Health and Safety at Work Act	
1975	Sex Discrimination Act (amended 1986)	
1976	Race Relations Act	Introduced concept of indirect discrimination
1982	Employment Act	
1983	Equal Pay (Amendment) Regulations	
1984	Data Protection Act	
1989	Employment Act	
1992	Trade Unions and Labour Relations (Consolidation) Act	
	Social Security Contributions and Benefits Acts	
1993	Trade Union Reform and Employment Rights Act	
1994	Statutory Sick Pay Act	
1995	Disability Discrimination Act	
1996	Employment Rights Act	
	Employment Tribunals Act	
1998	Employment Rights (Dispute Resolution) Act	
	Working Time Regulations	
	Data Protection Act	Implications for recruitment procedures
	Teaching and Higher Education Act	Time off work for study
	Public Interest Disclosure Act	Protects whistle-blowers
1999	Employment Relations Act	Union recognition
	Tax Credits Act	
	Collective Redundancies and Transfer of Undertakings (Amendment) Regulations	
	Maternity and Parental Leave Regulations	
2000	Part-time Workers (Prevention of Less Favourable Treatment) Regulations	
2001	Sex Discrimination (Indirect Discrimination and Burden of Proof) Regulations	
2002	Employment Bill	

significant increase in tribunal business. Since Labour returned to power in 1997, the pace has accelerated with the acceptance of the European Social Chapter and the government's own domestic employment policy initiatives.[1] We therefore have novel issues such as working time regulations, parental leave, the national minimum wage, and so on, with legislation outlawing discrimination on grounds of age, religion or sexual orientation also promised in the near future. And the recent incorporation into UK law of the European Convention on Human Rights[2] is already having an impact on tribunal applications.

The result of all this is that employment tribunals now have jurisdiction over more than eighty types of complaint. Table 1 shows the basic legislative structure for this jurisdiction, while Figure 1 shows the way in which total applications have risen since the 1980s. Many applications involve claims under more than one jurisdiction, and these have to be separately considered. For instance, someone who has lost his or her job may claim unfair dismissal, unfair deductions from pay and racial discrimination in one application. In 2000/01, there was an average of 1.7 jurisdictions per application; this figure was 1.4 three or four years previously.

The large number of applications needs to be seen in the context of a still larger number of disputes which do not make it as far as the application stage. ACAS receives about three-quarters of a million enquiries a year asking for advice about individual grievances, and the DTI has suggested that there may be up to 900,000

---

1 See Better Regulation Task Force, *Employment Regulation: striking a balance*, May 2002.

2 K. D. Ewing, 'The Human Rights Act and Labour Law', *Industrial Law Journal*, 27, 4, 1998, pp. 275–92.

Figure 1   **Registered tribunal applications, Great Britain**

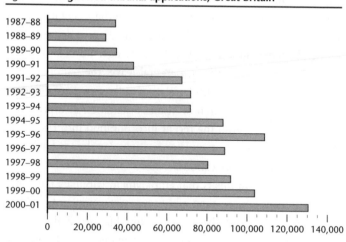

Source: Employment Tribunals Service.

disputes annually which could in principle lead to tribunal applications.[3]

Types of application

The pattern of applications to employment tribunals has changed over time. It is not easy to get comparable figures for different periods as there have been changes in law, as well as in reporting period and classification. Nevertheless, the figures in Table 2 show the broad picture.[4] They demonstrate that there has been

3   Department of Trade and Industry, *Routes to Resolution: Improving Dispute Resolution in Britain*, July 2001, p. 3.

4   For an explanation of the main categories of claims, see T. Brown, H. Mortlock, C. Rankin and A. T. Phillips, *Employment Tribunal Claims*, Stationery Office, London, 2000.

Table 2 **Categories of application as percentage of total**

	1985	1993–94	1997–98	2000–01
Unfair dismissal	73	61	47	46
Redundancy	12	12	7	5
Race discrimination	na	2	3	4
Sex discrimination/equal pay	na	4	6	6
Disability discrimination				2
[All discrimination]	[8]	[6]	[9]	[12]
Breach of contract			9	10
Unlawful deduction/Wages Act		16	20	20
Working time				1
Other	7	5	8	6
Total number of applications	38,590	71,661	80,435	130,408

Source: Own calculations from Employment Tribunals Service Annual Reports, *Labour Market Trends* (various dates); S. Burgess, C. Propper and D. Wilson, *Explaining the growth in the number of applications to Industrial Tribunals 1972–1997*, Department of Trade and Industry Employment Relations Research Series 10, 2001.

a decline over time in unfair dismissal and redundancy cases as a proportion of applications, though not in absolute terms.[5] This is partly the effect of the expansion of tribunal jurisdiction to new areas over time, but it also reflects cyclical factors. In a period of economic boom, there are fewer dismissals, for example, and thus fewer unfair dismissal claims.[6]

The table shows that applications relating to discrimination issues have become more important over time. These are the cases,

5 The figures in Table 2 are for 'main jurisdiction', i.e. the most important category of claim where, as explained earlier, individuals may be making more than one complaint.

6 An analysis of unfair dismissal claims over the period 1975–91 concluded that cyclical factors explained most of the variation in this type of claim. See S. Brown, B. Frick and J. Sessions, 'Unemployment, vacancies and unjust dismissals: the cyclical demand for individual grievance procedures in Germany and Great Britain', *Labour: Review of Labour Economics and Industrial Relations*, 11, 2, 1997, pp. 329–49.

like some of those quoted in Chapter 1, which have most often hit the headlines. However, such cases remain a relatively small proportion of all applications, way behind the numbers for less controversial questions concerning unlawful wage deductions and various breaches of the Wages Act.[7]

So cases have been growing, not only in number but also in complexity and range of jurisdiction. Although most cases are resolved before coming to a hearing, there is still a very substantial burden on the tribunal system and upon employers and employees. It is unsurprising that growing concern has been expressed about the working of the system, which has developed far beyond its modest beginnings.

How tribunals work

Tribunals are independent judicial bodies made up of a legally qualified chairperson and (normally) two 'lay' members.[8] The chairpersons, of whom there are around 100 full-time and 200 part-time, are people with legal qualifications and experience. They are appointed by the Lord Chancellor in England, and the Lord President of the Court of Session in Scotland. The lay members, following a case brought under the Human Rights Act,[9] are now appointed through open competition by the Secretary of State for Trade and Industry. They are appointed to two lists – one drawn from those with an employee perspective, the other from

7   These concern, for example, deductions from pay for stock deficiencies, issues about unpaid bonuses, statutory sick pay and maternity pay.

8   The chairpersons sit alone for some types of claims of a more technical nature, for instance those concerning unlawful deductions from wages.

9   *Smith v. Secretary of State for Trade and Industry*, 2000 (ICR 69).

employers. There are over 2,000 panel members in Great Britain; they have the legal right to time off work for tribunal service.

An individual wishing to make a claim fills in a standard form and sends it to the nearest Employment Tribunals Office; there are currently 33 of these. If the administration accepts that the case is within the jurisdiction of the system, it will be registered and details of the claim will be sent to the respondent.

Claims are usually made against an employer, but fellow employees can also be respondents (as in sexual harassment cases), as can trade unions (in a case where someone is unlawfully excluded from membership). Note also that 'employer' should be taken to include 'potential employer', as a firm that is alleged to discriminate in its recruitment procedure can be a respondent to a claim by a disappointed applicant with whom there is no contractual relationship. In 1995–97 23 per cent of discrimination cases related to job applications, with 62 per cent of these applicants not being employed by the organisation at the time of application.[10]

The respondent is required to make a written response to an application within three weeks. On the basis of this response, arrangements may be set in hand for a formal hearing. Before this, however, ACAS will receive details of the employee's claim and the employer's response. A conciliation officer will be appointed and will contact the parties, offering help to achieve a settlement. ACAS conciliation is a vital feature of the process. Well over a third of cases are settled in this way without coming before a formal tribunal: the system would otherwise be impossible to manage with current resources.

In fact only a minority of all cases – around 27 per cent in

---

10 Department of Trade and Industry, *Findings from the 1998 Survey of Employment Tribunal Applications*, DTI Employment Relations Research Series 13, 2002, p. 14.

Table 3 **Outcome of tribunal applications 2000/01**

Outcome	Percentage of applications
ACAS conciliated settlements	37
Withdrawn	29
Successful at tribunal hearing	15
Dismissed at hearing	12
Otherwise disposed of	7

Source: Employment Tribunals Service Annual Report.

2000/01 – eventually reach a tribunal hearing. As Table 3 shows, 29 per cent were withdrawn and 7 per cent were disposed of in other ways, for instance by private agreement.

The categories reported in official figures are not watertight. It appears, for example, that a large proportion of formally 'withdrawn' cases are in fact privately settled. When respondents and applicants are questioned separately, respondents are more likely to report a case withdrawn, and applicants to report one settled.[11]

The summary figures in Table 3 conceal considerable differences in the outcome of particular classes of application. While the table shows that 37 per cent of all applications were settled through ACAS, only 19 per cent of equal pay cases were settled in this way. Similarly, while 15 per cent of all applications were successful at tribunal, this hides a variation between 30 per cent of redundancy cases and only 1 per cent of equal pay cases (66 per cent of which, however, were withdrawn). Variations in the percentage outcomes depend on such factors as the complexity of the legislation on particular jurisdictions, the likely scale of compensation and the nature of the evidence required.

11   Ibid., Chapter 7.

Tribunal hearings, held in ETS buildings or hired premises around the country, are meant to be relatively informal, although they follow legal procedures including giving evidence on oath. When they began it was hoped that both employees and employers would dispense with legal representation. This proved over-optimistic. There is currently no legal aid for conducting tribunal cases in England and Wales (though there is in Scotland), but funds are available for preparing a case. ETS data show that there are considerable fluctuations in the extent of legal representation from year to year, but on average around 20 per cent of applicants are legally represented,[12] and a larger proportion of employers.

Professionalisation of the procedure is also enhanced by earlier consultation with solicitors; 49 per cent of applicants consult a solicitor, while 63 per cent of employers discuss the case with an external law firm – and many larger firms have in-house legal expertise.[13] Many applicants also draw on union assistance and/or the help of Citizens Advice Bureaux. In discrimination and equal pay cases, the Commission for Racial Equality, the Disability Rights Commission and the Equal Opportunities Commission frequently play a role. On the employer's side, larger firms will employ specialist personnel advisers; in some industries employers' associations are involved. All this external assistance means that less than a third of either applicants or respondents are obliged or choose to represent themselves.

---

12 Some lawyers have begun to offer representation on an American-style 'no win, no fee' basis.

13 Department of Trade and Industry, op. cit., Chapter 5.

At the tribunal

In an anonymous room with dingy institutional paint, tired lace curtains and poor ventilation, the three middle-aged tribunal members sit behind desks arranged in an arc. Their coats (for it is a winter morning) hang on pegs behind them. The legal representative has a chair that appears to be larger than those of her colleagues. This is presumably meant to add to her authority, for I have noticed the same feature at other tribunals. In fact the effect is unimpressive, for her chair seems to be the same kind of standard shabby office furniture as those of her colleagues, with the simple added feature of a headrest.

Two of the tribunal members are scribbling furiously as they listen intently to the evidence. The third has entered the computer age and is typing equally furiously into a laptop. All three are concentrating hard, giving spectators the impression that they are scowling. There is no eye contact with the witness.

This is the second day of a racial discrimination case, which the clerk tells me is expected to last three days. The witness currently giving evidence is sitting to the panel's right and facing into the court. In front of her is an old-fashioned Bible, a thick ring binder referred to in lawyerspeak as a 'bundle', and a glass of water.

The witness, who is not the respondent, has been there for 45 minutes, during which time she has struggled to recall events and conversations dating back four years. The applicant's representative is a trade union official with much experience in these matters. He questions the witness closely. Visibly perspiring, she offers an elaborate opinion in response to an awkward question. The chair of the tribunal suddenly looks up and abruptly snaps, 'Just answer "yes" or "no", please.' This disconcerts the witness, who looks even more worried. The two parties' representatives whisper in the ears of colleagues ranged along tables facing the tribunal. Behind them, on four rows of uncomfortable plastic seats, are the applicant and his wife, and two other people sitting apart. They may be involved in the case, or perhaps, like me, they are merely observers. Tribunals are, after all, public courts.

The respondent's lawyer now takes up the questioning. As is so often the way in race discrimination applications, the respondent is represented by a minority lawyer; next door, in a sex discrimination case, the employer is being represented by a woman. Whether such a transparent strategy benefits respondents is doubtful, however.

In this instance, the respondent's lawyer refers frequently to the bundle of documents relating to the case. 'Please look at the e-mail which you sent to the applicant on September twentieth. You'll find this on page 324. Have you got it?' He is interrupted by the tribunal chair, who has lost her place. When everyone has found the relevant page, we continue. 'Now what does this reference to poor timekeeping refer to?'

When the representatives of the two parties have had their fill, the two lay members of the tribunal break their silence and ask a couple of further questions. The witness is asked to spell a name. The chair then calls a halt, to the palpable relief of the witness. The hearing will resume after lunch, when another witness is expected.

Compensation

Following a tribunal award, the consequences depend on the particular legislation covering the claim. In cases of unfair dismissal, *reinstatement* (restoration to the same job) or *re-engagement* (transfer to a different job with the same employer) may be possible. These outcomes are, however, extremely rare. There were only 15 examples of reinstatement or re-engagement in the 5,294 unfair dismissal applications upheld by tribunals in 2000/01.[14]

This contrasts with countries such as Germany and Italy, where reinstatement after a finding of unfair dismissal is mandatory. Interestingly, British unions are currently pressing for compulsory reinstatement,[15] while simultaneously the Italian government has created a furore by trying to remove this provision from Italian labour law. The practical problems of reinstating an individual with whom relations have irretrievably broken down make employers very hostile to provisions of this kind.

Compensation is, then, the usual outcome of a successful tribunal claim. This is calculated according to different formulae for different types of claim. For unfair dismissal there is an inflation-linked upper limit to compensation, but for discrimination cases there are no upper limits. At the time of writing, the record for a sex discrimination award stands at £1.4 million, with the highest race discrimination payment standing at just over £800,000.

It is also possible for *costs* to be awarded to a successful complainant (and also against a vexatious one),[16] but this is very

14　Employment Tribunals Service Annual Report.

15　Patience Wheatcroft, 'Addressing the state of the union', *The Times*, 11 June 2002.

16　'Vexatious' cases are probably fairly small in number. The 1998 Survey of Employment Tribunal Applications suggests a definition of a vexatious application as one where the applicant has rejected professional advice to withdraw a claim.

Table 4 **Compensation awarded by employment tribunals, 2000/01 (£)**

	Mean	Median	Highest award
Unfair dismissal	5,122	2,744	69,912*
Race discrimination	15,484	8,012	201,260
Sex discrimination	11,024	5,499	139,896
Disability discrimination	12,978	5,000	71,063

* The amount that could be awarded under this heading was capped during
this financial year at £51,700 plus a 'basic' award of the statutory redundancy
entitlement. Compensation in the discrimination categories is unlimited.
Source: Employment Tribunals Service Annual Report.

uncommon. Only 247 cost awards were made in total (to either
applicants or respondents) in 2000/01: the average award was just
£295, and only two were for over £1,000.[17]

An impression of the scale of compensation awarded can be
obtained from Table 4. The figures for highest awards can be
misleading, as they represent very unusual cases. In 1998–99, for
example, one of the biggest compensation awards went to football
manager Kenny Dalglish following the loss of his job at Newcastle
United: such cases are obviously atypical.

Nevertheless, the size of awards has been increasing in recent
years, particularly in discrimination cases. For example, ETS
Annual Reports show that the median award for race discrimination cases rose from £3,499 in 1993/94 to £4,555 in 1997/98 and
£8,012 in 2000/01.

If either party is dissatisfied with the outcome of the tribunal,
there is a limited ability to appeal on points of fact rather than

---

Only 4 per cent of cases in the 1998 survey met this criterion. However, even this
proportion may be an exaggeration, as in a fifth of these supposedly vexatious
cases the applicant went on to win at a full tribunal hearing.

17   Employment Tribunals Service Annual Report.

opinion. An Employment Appeals Tribunal, sitting in London and Edinburgh, consists of a judge and two lay members. As with employment tribunal applications, the number of cases going to appeal has risen sharply.[18] In 2000/01 the Employment Appeals Tribunal sat on 970 occasions, disposing of a total of 1,608 appeals. In 1993/94, by contrast, only 599 appeals were disposed of.

18 Legal aid is available for Employment Appeals Tribunal cases, and over half of applicants to the EAT are now represented by lawyers. Twenty-five years ago, the proportion was only 6 per cent. See S. Denman, 'Employment tribunals are just the job for m'learned friends', *Sunday Times*, 4 November 2001.

3 THE RISE OF THE TRIBUNALS

Why have tribunals grown so much in importance in the last 35 years? There seems to have been a fundamental change in the way in which politicians and the public think about the role of law in labour markets. The enormous range of legislative constraints now surrounding employment contracts needs some brief theoretical discussion, as well as a historical treatment.

No freedom of contract

Liberal economists have traditionally had a predilection for the notion of freedom of labour contract, the 'contract at will'.[1] In a complex modern economy like that of the United Kingdom there are hundreds of thousands of potential job opportunities available at any time. If people (employers and employees) voluntarily enter into a particular employment contract, this is evidence that they prefer this option to any other *which is currently on offer to them.*[2] It is a core belief of economics that both parties gain from a voluntary contract.

---

1   See R. A. Epstein, *Forbidden Grounds: The Case against Employment Discrimination Laws*, Harvard University Press, Cambridge, Mass., 1995, Chapter 8.

2   A crucial qualification. Clearly many people would prefer a better job than they currently have, but the point is that they are presumably doing the best they can for themselves at the moment by taking this employment opportunity.

In a free market, employment contracts will be of varying length, and involve very different rates of pay and conditions, depending on demand and supply factors. Because circumstances change over time, it seems reasonable to allow both parties to opt out of the arrangement at a later date without too much difficulty, subject to clear understanding on both sides about such matters as periods of notice and any agreed compensation. Firms and individuals can often improve their welfare by recontracting with other partners as new information and opportunities become available. It seems to follow that they should not be prevented from doing so by outside agencies, whether governments, labour unions, trade associations or professional bodies. In this view, a genuinely free labour market maximises both efficiency and personal freedom.

This view is widely held in relation to the employee's side of the bargain. There are very few restrictions placed on employees' freedom to quit their jobs, and movement to a better-paid job is seen as natural and even to be commended. As a result, even periods of notice stipulated in contracts are widely ignored. On the other side of the bargain, however, things are very different. Employers' freedom to terminate contracts is subject to considerable restrictions in this country and elsewhere in Europe,[3] *and it is not possible to negotiate exemptions from these restrictions which will hold up in court.* For example, in a recent case an engineering firm thought it had struck a deal by which, in return for higher pay, workers would become 'independent contractors', with no rights

---

3   There is still rather greater freedom to terminate contracts in the United States, where only around 10 per cent of workers have employment contracts that limit an employer's right to dismiss them. However, some other types of interference with freedom of contract, in relation, for example, to racial and sexual discrimination, are arguably greater in the USA than in Europe. See 'Women in Suits', *Economist*, 2 March 2002.

to redundancy pay. When, as a result of a downturn in demand, workers were laid off, one of them took his case to an employment tribunal – and won.[4]

This company was being naive, in view of the existing state of the law, but it is probably not alone in asking why it should not be possible to negotiate a deal which *ex ante* benefits both parties, albeit one with some risk of an unfavourable outcome. Isn't this what markets are all about?

One answer is to say that economists have long been aware that there may be elements of 'market failure' which justify some government interference with complete freedom of contract. Strictly speaking, a formal demonstration of the efficiency of a free competitive market depends on a set of textbook assumptions, such as full information, free entry to and exit from markets, and so forth. Market failure is said to arise when these conditions are not fully met, and it is claimed that government action to deal with the problem can in principle improve economic welfare.[5]

Examples of possible market failure in the formation of employment contracts might include *information imperfections and asymmetries* that arise in the work environment. Suppose that an employer knows that a production process involves the emission of fumes that damage employees' health, but the employees do not. It is plausible to argue that, if the employees knew of the health hazard, they might be unwilling to work at that particular job. There may therefore be a role for some government involvement

---

4   Reported in the *Daily Telegraph*, 5 September 2001.
5   Critics retort that market failure is an extremely slippery concept which should always be seen in relation to the symmetrical concept of 'government failure', where the conditions for perfect government are unmet. Opinions will, of course, differ as to which type of failure is more common.

to mitigate the problem, although this does not necessarily mean that the process should be banned or the employer punished.[6] Similarly, this sort of reasoning might justify some restrictions on the use of child labour, as minors are generally deemed incapable of fully understanding the options open to them, particularly in relation to education and future careers.

Other economic rationalisations for legal intervention in labour markets include the possibility of *positive externalities* (such as better socialisation and education of the next generation) resulting from parental leave, *second-best* arguments for severance pay (in the absence of private unemployment insurance markets where moral hazard problems arise) or action to offset *excessive market power* exercised by employers or groups of employees.[7]

Take the latter example. Single ('monopsonistic') employers in isolated areas, or in highly segmented labour markets for particular skills, or in new employment fields where competition is as yet limited, may be able to use their market position to force wages down below the competitive level. Conversely, powerful trade unions, or for that matter professional-membership bodies such

---

6 An alternative compatible with liberal economics might be to require full information to be provided to the employee. If he or she then chose to carry on working it would be because, the health evidence notwithstanding, continuing with the job was still the preferred option: many employees are quite prepared to undertake dangerous jobs if the pay is sufficient. This sort of reasoning justifies, in another field, a requirement for cigarettes to carry a health warning but nevertheless to be freely available. However, this apparently sensible solution is being rapidly undermined in the United States by juries' willingness to impose massive compensation for lifelong smokers who knew quite well the risks they were running.

7 For a discussion, see J. T. Addison and W. S. Siebert, *Regulating European Labour Markets: More costs than benefits?*, Hobart Paper 138, Institute of Economic Affairs, 1999, pp. 40–52.

as those dominating legal and medical occupations, may use their monopoly power in the labour market to raise wages and salaries to excessive levels by restricting competition from new job market entrants. Intervention to redress imbalances of market power has historically found much support amongst economists.

But a look at the range of jurisdictions of today's employment tribunals makes it clear that the economist's notion of market failure, however eclectically conceived, in reality explains remarkably little of the pattern of government intervention. Even in those areas where a rationale can be constructed, it is arguable that the case for intervention has declined over time. Knowledge about working conditions and environmental risks, for example, is now widespread. Globalisation, technical change and increasing movements of labour across borders have greatly reduced monopoly or monopsony powers in employment markets. And yet, far from there being a movement towards greater freedom of contract, labour market regulation continues to grow apace.

Few of the newer areas of state involvement – such as minimum wages, equal pay, racial and sexual discrimination, and working-time regulation – can easily be rationalised in terms of market failure in the economist's sense. They arise primarily from a continuing popular belief in the 'unfairness' of labour market outcomes. Rather than employers being seen as benefactors, providing the opportunity for people to improve their living standards and quality of life, they are seen as actual or potential exploiters of people. Employees therefore need protection – not only against their employers, but also against themselves and their fellow employees, for in moments of weakness they might be tempted to collude with their bosses (as in the engineering company case alluded to earlier).

It could be argued that such a perception has increased over time simply because the UK has become a richer, less deferential and better-educated society, and thus less willing to tolerate un-fairness which was previously accepted as a fact of life. However, that would be simplistic. There are many other factors at work.

Goodbye to Kahn-Freund

It now requires a considerable effort of will to remember that, not so very long ago, government interference in the UK labour market was as unpopular with politicians, academics and organ-ised employees as it remains with John Monks's 'bad bosses'. In the 1950s and early 1960s it was a commonplace in discussions of labour relations in the UK that, in the words of Otto Kahn-Freund, the doyen of industrial relations specialists: 'There is, perhaps, no major country in the world in which the law has played a less significant role … and in which today the law and the legal profes-sion have less to do with labour relations.'[8]

Indeed, with the important exceptions of factory legislation and the Wages Councils,[9] there was very little direct involve-ment of government in the labour market. Unlike continental Europe, where Catholic social concern and what has been called the 'Roman-Germanic' tradition of activist government mean that there is a long history of labour market regulation, the UK scene was one where the government traditionally took a back seat. The

---

8   A. Flanders and H. Clegg (eds), *The System of Industrial Relations in Great Britain*, Basil Blackwell, Oxford, 1954, p. 44.

9   Factory legislation dates back to the middle of the nineteenth century, and the antecedents of the Wages Councils to the Liberal government's regulation of the 'sweated trades' in the first decades of the twentieth century.

country was not a member of the European Community, which had anyway not yet acquired the power, or even very much pretension, to regulate labour markets. Furthermore, despite the heavy involvement of British civil servants and trade union officials in the creation of the International Labour Organisation (ILO), both Conservative and Labour governments were for many years very reluctant to ratify ILO conventions which would have required legislation.[10]

This absence of direct government interference did not mean that the labour market was characterised by perfect competition; far from it. Trade unions were powerful, in large part because of government-granted immunities against damages resulting from strikes, and the consensus of the time was that a regime of 'free collective bargaining' was sufficient to protect the worker from employer excesses. To trade union leaders, but also to writers such as Kahn-Freund and the Oxford School of industrial relations theorists,[11] the use of the law in labour markets was very much a poor second to collective bargaining. It was to be used only when unions were weak. Even then, as in the case of Wages Councils (where the government set pay minima for 'unorganised' industries), the aim was to build trade union membership up to the level where direct government intervention could be dispensed with.

The Oxford School believed in a pluralistic approach to management–labour relations where workers in trade unions

---

10 P. Davies and M. Freedland, *Labour Legislation and Public Policy*, Clarendon Press, Oxford, 1993, p. 25. The International Labour Organisation was founded in the aftermath of World War I, in part to head off the danger of social unrest and revolution by promoting minimum labour standards.

11 Including such influential figures as Hugh Clegg (who, together with Kahn-Freund, served on the Donovan Commission on trade union reform from 1965 to 1968), Allan Flanders and Alan Fox.

had a collective right to 'jointly regulate' pay and conditions with employers, who would preferably themselves be organised in employers' associations covering large industries. In economists' terms the ideal, therefore, seems to have been a monopoly trade union facing a monopsonistic employers' association. However, that is not how the Oxford writers, whose members were either innocent of economic analysis or scornful of it, conceptualised matters.

The Oxford School tended to idealise trade unions as a legitimate power in the land. This was partly the result of World War II, during which the leading trade unionist Ernest Bevin served as Minister of Labour and unions were accorded establishment respectability. A residue of the war years, however, was a powerful shop steward movement with considerable disruptive potential. The Oxford School writers wanted to import greater order into UK industry by extending collective bargaining and increasing the power of union officials at the expense of the shop stewards, who were implicated in the large number of unofficial strikes in the 1960s.

Some other academics, most notably Friedrich Hayek, took a different view, seeing unions not as legitimate agents of order but rather as 'uniquely privileged institutions to which the general rules of law do not apply', using their position to coerce individual workers and employers.[12] Hayek argued for the unions' legal immunities from damages claims to be removed and institutions such as the 'closed shop' to be dismantled. His influence was very limited at that time, however, though his analysis of trade union-

---

12 F. A. Hayek, *The Constitution of Liberty*, Routledge and Kegan Paul, London, 1960, pp. 267–8.

ism was to become a key influence on the Thatcher government's thinking in the 1980s.[13]

Nevertheless, by the late 1960s it was being increasingly felt by politicians and the public that unions were becoming too powerful, using the strike weapon promiscuously to force inflationary pay settlements on employers.[14] The Labour government of the day used incomes policy as a temporary expedient in the attempt to control inflation, but also set up the Donovan Commission to consider reform of the industrial relations set-up. When this long-winded inquiry produced an anodyne report,[15] the Wilson administration nevertheless proceeded to a more radical stance with the ill-fated *In Place of Strife* proposals. The failure of this attempt at reform, and that of the Heath government's Industrial Relations Act, set the scene for a further growth in union power in the 1970s, culminating in the notorious 'Winter of Discontent' which ushered in the Thatcher years.

The tide then turned, with the Conservatives embarking on a long series of legislative reforms which played an important part in reducing the power of trade unions.[16] Together with other factors, such as the recessions of the early 1980s and 1990s, declines

---

13 See S. Auerbach, 'Mrs Thatcher's Labour Laws: Slouching Towards Utopia?', *Political Quarterly*, January–March 1993, pp. 37–48.

14 This is not to deny the monetarist explanation of inflation as the result of over-expansion of the money supply. Such monetary incontinence was arguably a reaction by governments to pressure for excessive wage settlements which would otherwise have resulted in unemployment.

15 Interestingly in the present context, however, Donovan argued for an expansion of the role of the fledgling industrial tribunals and their renaming as 'labour tribunals'. See *Royal Commission on Trade Unions and Employers Associations 1965–1968 Report*, Cmnd 3623, 1968, Chapter X.

16 See J. R. Shackleton, 'Industrial Relations Reform in Britain since 1979', *Journal of Labor Research*, summer 1998, pp. 581–605.

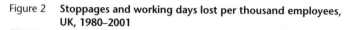

Figure 2   **Stoppages and working days lost per thousand employees, UK, 1980–2001**

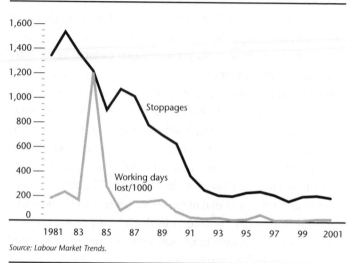

Source: Labour Market Trends.

in traditionally heavily unionised industries and the changing gender composition of the workforce, these reforms were associated with a decline in union membership from well over 13 million (53 per cent of all employees) in 1979 to around 7 million (less than 30 per cent of employees) at the end of the 1990s. Figure 2 demonstrates the implications of this decline in trade union strength for indicators of collective disputes. Although there has recently been a mild resurgence of strikes on the railways and elsewhere, industrial militancy remains far below the levels reached in the 1970s and early 1980s.

Individual rather than collective rights

The subduing of the unions has been seen by admirers of the
Thatcher governments as one of their greatest achievements, the
fulfilment of a desire going back many years. But folklore tells us
to be careful what we wish for: those who get their wishes granted
often find they have got something they did not quite bargain for.
The new focus on individual rights manifested in the growth of
tribunal applications is the flipside of the decline in union power.
Casual comparison of Figures 1 and 2 shows that total applications
to tribunals rose broadly as industrial stoppages fell. More con-
vincingly, disaggregated analysis of tribunal applications shows
that the decline in union membership is statistically associated
with a rise in several individual categories of application, notably
those concerned with breaches of the Wages Act.[17]

Why is this the case? As early as the 1971 Industrial Relations
Act, the Conservative government under Edward Heath had introduced legal redress for unfair dismissal in order to try to reduce
the number of unofficial strikes caused by workers being sacked.
Later, under Margaret Thatcher, the Conservatives made great
play of asserting *individual* rather than *collective* 'rights'[18] in their
labour market reforms. The right not to belong to a trade union,
the right to ballots and the right to inspect union accounts were
obvious examples of this. Interestingly, the Conservatives also
used their eight major pieces of employment legislation between

---

17   See S. Burgess, C. Propper and D. Wilson, *Explaining the growth in the number of applications to Industrial Tribunals 1972–1997*, Department of Trade and Industry Employment Relations Research Series 10, 2001.

18   W. Brown, S. Deakin, D. Nash and S. Oxenbridge, 'The Employment Contract: From Collective Procedures to Individual Rights', *British Journal of Industrial Relations*, 38, 4, December 2000, pp. 611–29.

1980 and 1993 to slip into law various European directives which required them to extend individual rights in the labour market, for example widening the coverage of sex discrimination law and maternity leave. This conflation of different types of legislation made the anti-union measures more palatable to employees. By the same token, anti-Brussels, Conservative trade union reformers had to accept legislation relating to European directives relating to individual rights.

Another reason for the association between the decline of unions and the move to assertion of individual rights in the labour market was the result of the changing composition of the workforce. The traditional union battalions – the miners, the dockers – were 100 per cent male and virtually 100 per cent white. In their heyday, unions could lay claim to a collective solidarity based on social homogeneity and common economic interests. But the 1980s and 1990s were marked by great changes in the workforce. As a result, women now constitute nearly half of those in work, and ethnic minorities account for around 10 per cent, with the proportion being significantly higher in the younger age groups.

With this more diverse workforce, it is difficult to assert traditional union solidarity while women earn less than men within the same union, and some (though not all) ethnic minorities have markedly lower pay and a much higher probability of becoming unemployed than whites. It is hardly surprising that these disadvantaged groups have favoured the extension of equal pay and discrimination legislation, rather than continued reliance on the 'joint regulation' of pay and conditions between employers and unions favoured by earlier generations of workers. They make use of the law in increasing numbers. It has been demonstrated that demographic changes play a statistically significant role in explaining the growth of discrimination applications.[19]

Unions and tribunals

Trade unions have, inevitably, adjusted to the wasting of their industrial muscle. Many of the more successful unions have fought back by selling themselves to employers and government as sensible, responsible partners in a new industrial settlement. They have merged to gain economies of scale, enabling them to market themselves to potential members on the basis of a range of services, including cheap insurance, holiday deals, healthcare – but also including representation at tribunals. Legal services are generally regarded as being among the most attractive selling points to new union members.[20]

Some unions go farther and actively encourage individuals whose cases form part of what is, in effect, a class action against employers. The aim is to achieve through employment tribunals what can no longer be achieved through strikes: 'trade unions use multiple applications on the same individual issue as a way of pursuing a collective issue'.[21] For instance, in September 2001 the Public and Commercial Services Union announced that it planned to instigate up to 20 equal pay cases in an attempt to force the Department for Environment, Food and Rural Affairs to grant higher pay to all their members to bring them into line with other government departments.[22]

19 Burgess, Propper and Wilson, op.cit.
20 'See you in court, say unions', *Labour Research*, February 2000, pp. 17–18.
21 Y. Bennion and A. Rogers, *Courts or Compromise?*, Industrial Society policy paper, February 2001, p. 2.
22 D. Gow, 'Union pushes for equal pay at DEFRA', *Guardian*, 29 September 2001.

Table 5 **Union criteria for supporting claims**

Criterion	Percentage affected
Where the chance of success appears high	81
Based on lawyers' recommendations	77
Where a significant number of members are affected	55
Where a principle of law is involved	52
As a result of, or in anticipation of, a change in the law	32
Depends on cost	29
No specific criteria	10

Source: TUC, *Focus on Employment Tribunals,* February 2001.

So unions are very active players in employment tribunals. They are, however, selective. The proportion of applications supported by unions has fluctuated considerably from year to year and shows no clear trend. Decisions to support members in a particular application seem to have been increasingly devolved: 65 per cent of unions responding to a TUC survey in 2000 reported that a decision to support a claim was taken at the level of full-time officials, rather than at committee or national executive level, as against only 46 per cent a year previously. Only 16 per cent of unions said that general secretaries or executive bodies made such decisions, although top-level decision-making was much more important when it came to supporting appeals. Table 5 shows the reasons that union respondents gave for supporting particular cases.

Selectivity seems to pay off. Whereas around half of all employees appearing at a tribunal hearing are successful, the figure for union-represented applicants is as high as 83 per cent. They also receive higher settlements. In unfair dismissal cases, for example, union-supported applicants received awards that were more than double the average for all successful claims.[23]

23   TUC, *Focus on Employment Tribunals,* February 2001.

The rest of Europe

Success at tribunals means that union officials have increasingly looked to the EU to achieve gains for their members. They saw throughout the 1980s and 1990s a steady increase in social legislation coming from Brussels, much of it within the Trojan horse of the 1986 Single European Act. This process has been accelerated since the acceptance of the Social Chapter agenda in the Treaty of Amsterdam.[24]

Interpretations of existing law by the European Court of Justice have also extended the scope of employment tribunals in ways that favour employees. Examples include the requirement for part-time employees to be given access to occupational pensions,[25] and recent decisions relating to the Transfer of Undertakings, the latter an important area for the UK, where merger and demerger are much easier than elsewhere in the EU, and where there has been a big increase in outsourcing.[26] One writer comments:

> … the European Court of Justice continues to give rulings
> in employment law cases which have a profound effect
> on national legal systems. This places a heavy burden on
> national courts and tribunals. They must interpret national
> legislation, and reconcile it with rulings of the ECJ, whilst

---

24 The process by which the EU has acquired increasing powers to regulate labour markets is traced in Addison and Siebert, op. cit.

25 The 1994 European Court of Justice ruling on this has proved expensive for UK employers. It has led to the further House of Lords judgment that enables part-timers to backdate their claims to 1976, a form of retrospection which could in principle cost many billions of pounds. 'Part-timers' claims may cost £17 billion', *The Times*, 10 February 2001.

26 Where a business or part of a business is transferred as a recognisable entity to a new owner, the new employer is obliged to maintain most of the existing terms and conditions of service.

> still remaining within the realm of interpreting, as opposed
> to rewriting or overruling ... This problem is particularly
> acute for Great Britain, because it is a common law country
> with a long history of well-established traditions and special
> circumstances.[27]

Mention of the EU is an occasion for pointing out that Britain is by no means alone in having large numbers of individual employees claiming redress under an ever-expanding range of laws and regulations.[28] In continental Europe the Roman-Germanic tradition has favoured comprehensive labour legislation for many years, with rights usually exercised through some sort of tribunal.

For example, in Germany tripartite labour courts settle conflicts arising from the employment relationship. The system comprises local labour courts, higher labour courts at the *Land* (state) level and a Federal Labour Court. In France the *conseils de prud'hommes* deal with individual disputes. Here the judges are elected by employers represented in employers' associations and employees from unions and other groups. In Belgium 'social judges', representing employers and employees, sit alongside professional judges. In Luxembourg a labour tribunal consists of a presiding magistrate and two assessors, one chosen from an employer panel and one from an employee panel appointed by the Ministry of Justice on the advice of the Ministry of Labour.

Across many European countries there is a similar experience of a large and expanding case load, in some cases threatening to overload the system; in Italy in the late 1990s, for example, there

---

27 R. Singh, 'European Community Employment Law: Key recent cases and their implications for the UK', *Industrial Relations Journal*, 30, 4, 2000, p. 385.

28 For a discussion see C. Barnard, J. Clark and R. Lewis, *The exercise of individual employment rights in the member states of the European Community*, Department of Employment Research Series No. 49, 1995.

were said to be around one million cases pending. In Ireland there was a 19 per cent increase in claims and appeals in 2000.[29]

The incidence of cases, indeed, seems to be higher in most other major European countries than in Britain. Thus in Germany there were 594,000 new cases brought before the local labour courts in 1998. About half of these cases concerned unfair dismissal with around 35 per cent concerning pay issues, a not uncommon pattern. Unfair dismissal is a wider concept in several EU countries than it is in the UK, as Marks & Spencer discovered to its cost when it tried to close its French stores.[30] Thus German employers need to consult works councils before making redundancies, and must observe 'social considerations' when selecting for redundancy. This means that they must examine whether someone selected deserves less social protection than comparable employees, with the criteria including length of service, age and family responsibilities. Anybody 'unfairly' selected for redundancy can bring a case for reinstatement. Similar provisions apply in Sweden.

Schneider[31] points out that there was an explosion of claims in eastern Germany following reunification. He puts this down to the collapse of trade union membership in the East and the uncertainty about the meaning of new labour legislation.

Despite the pressures of rising numbers of claims, however, there is still a considerable appetite for further regulation of the labour market in continental Europe. Ever since the Maastricht

---

29   *Irish Times*, 25 November 2001.

30   C. Birkinshaw and M. Fairclough, 'Employee rights and management wrongs', *Financial Times*, 26 November 2001.

31   M. Schneider, 'What Do Labour Courts Do? Evidence from the Eastern German Transformation', paper presented at the European Association of Labour Economists/Society of Labour Economists World Conference, Milan, June 2000.

Treaty there has been a perception that the Single Market requires a common system of rules to avoid what is called 'social dumping' – firms moving around the EU in search of less restrictive labour market regulation. There is no real sign of the Commission losing enthusiasm for this issue, in terms of which the UK is still perceived as a laggard despite signing up to the Social Chapter. It seems likely that there will continue to be new forms of regulation coming forward from the EU, with change and uncertainty the prospect for employers for the foreseeable future.

The economics of uncertainty and the rise of tribunal applications

The issue of uncertainty merits discussion. It needs setting in the context of decision-making by employers and employees.

Economic reasoning suggests that employees considering taking a case to a tribunal will do so if the *expected benefits* exceed the *expected costs*. Expected benefits are determined by the rewards to the employee (tribunal awards, and the subjective value of obtaining justice and, perhaps, exposing the employer to adverse publicity) from a successful application, and the probability of succeeding in the application. An increase in the value of typical awards or an increase in the probability of success have been shown, other things being equal, to increase the number of tribunal applications (after a time lag while information is disseminated).[32] Expected costs to employees include legal costs, the

---

32 Although the relative importance of size of award and probability of success seems to vary between jurisdictions. Probability of success is more important for unfair dismissal cases, with size of award more important for discrimination applications. See Burgess, Propper and Wilson, op. cit.

possible damage to an employee's future employment prospects and the less quantifiable costs of stress – all weighted by the probability of incurring these costs.

On the employer's side, the issues are a little more complicated. An employer considering whether or not to comply with an employment regulation will weigh the expected costs of compliance against the costs of non-compliance. The costs of compliance (for example, granting parental leave) are likely to be significant, for otherwise employers would be willing to offer a benefit without legislative pressure. In the case of non-compliance there will be penalties attached if an employee brings a tribunal case. These may be monetary or reputational. In reaching a decision as to whether or not to comply, the employer will be affected by the probability of a successful application being brought.

It may be objected that few employees or employers sit down to evaluate alternatives in this way. True, but this is a similar objection to that raised against the economist's characterisation of consumer choice as a rational process. Nevertheless, there is plenty of evidence to support the view that consumers in practice behave *as if* they were evaluating the marginal utility of an extra purchase; by the same token, employers and employees on average behave rationally to a far greater extent than critics realise.

Where does uncertainty come in? If we lived in a world where the costs and benefits, and their associated probabilities, were stable and known, the degree of compliance and the associated level of tribunal applications would surely settle down to an equilibrium position, in rather the same way as the forces of supply and demand in a market determine equilibrium price and output. If, on the other hand, employers do not clearly understand the extent of their legal obligations, or if employees believe that their rights are greater than they are in reality, there is likely to be a high level of applications. In such circumstances, fuller information and greater clarity in the law would be expected to lead to a fall in applications.

This is an analysis that draws an analogy with a long-established literature on the economics of strikes – the manifestation of collective rather than individual disputes. Many years ago the Nobel Prize-winning economist Sir John Hicks wrote that 'the majority of actual strikes are … the result of faulty negotiation … adequate knowledge will always make a settlement possible'.[33] More recently, this insight was developed by Stanley Siebert and John Addison into an analysis of strikes as 'accidents' produced by uncertainties in the bargaining process. If unions and employers could foresee exactly how a strike would end, both parties would have an incentive not to enter the strike – because strikes impose costs on both parties, a settlement would always be possible and preferable. The conclusion drawn by Siebert and Addison is that 'measures to reduce strikes should take the form of attempts to bring greater certainty into the relations between management and labour'.[34]

Equivalently, if the results of tribunal applications were known with greater certainty, we might expect their numbers to fall. Employers would know what was required for compliance, and employees would know clearly what their rights were and would not engage in speculative applications with little chance of success. However, the legal environment is *not* stable, and has become increasingly unpredictable in recent years. William Sargent, of the

33 J. R. Hicks, *The Theory of Wages* (2nd ed.), Macmillan, London, 1963, pp. 146–7.
34 W. S. Siebert and J. T. Addison, 'Are Strikes Accidental?', *Economic Journal*, 91, June 1981, p. 403.

government's advisory Small Business Council, regards tribunal outcomes as a lottery: 'Lawyers will tell you that, even if the facts are straightforward, the result ... is unpredictable.'[35]

Employment law is frequently changing, and the multiple levels of legislation and legal interpretation in the UK and the EU, noted earlier, mean that employers are often deeply unclear about their obligations. Employees, meanwhile, may, as a result of sensationalised press reports, develop an exaggerated view of their legal rights and the probability of their tribunal success.[36] Fuelled by stories of large pay-outs, some employees may indeed be tempted to 'take a punt', in Digby Jones's words. Pervasive uncertainty is also likely to be another reason why employers claim that they feel obliged to pay off tribunal applicants before a hearing occurs, even when they feel that they are in the right: better not to take the risk.

In time, as knowledge of rewards, penalties and probabilities improves, tribunal applications might be expected to fall – but this will only happen when the legal environment settles down. At the moment there is little sign of this occurring.

It is very difficult for even the fairest-minded and most conscientious employer to understand the implications of new employment legislation.

Take, for instance, the issue of the burden of proof in sex discrimination cases. Previously, aggrieved employees had to demonstrate that a particular employment practice acted to discriminate

---

35 K. Brown and C. Adams, 'The jury is out over tribunal reform plan', *Financial Times*, 15 November 2001.

36 The British Chambers of Commerce have called for an information campaign 'to smash the myth of huge payouts' which they believe is one factor driving the growth of tribunal applications. See BCC press release, 3 November 2000.

Burden of proof, Type I and Type II errors and optimal enforcement

Despite anti-discrimination legislation having been in operation for many years, there are still significant labour market inequalities between men and women, and between the white majority and some ethnic minorities. These are manifested in pay differences, employment patterns, unemployment rates, hours worked and many other ways. It is held by, for example, the Equal Opportunities Commission and the Commission for Racial Equality that a large proportion of the disadvantage suffered by particular groups is explained by continuing discrimination. It is argued that the difficulties of proving any but the most overt discrimination justify reversing the traditional burden of proof. Where an employment rule appears to have what the American courts call 'disparate impact' on groups of workers, we should therefore assume that the rule is discriminatory unless the employer can prove otherwise, by, for example, showing it is a necessary condition of employment.

If an employer insists that all cleaners should possess five GCSEs, this would favour those ethnic groups with high levels of academic achievement over those with poorer achievement. Since GCSEs are not necessary to be a competent cleaner, the qualifications requirement could be judged to be discriminatory. This might seem fairly clear cut, but what about a university requiring applicants for a lectureship to possess a PhD? It could be argued that it is not strictly necessary to possess a doctorate to teach and conduct competent research. If more men than women possess a doctorate, does this make most UK universities guilty of discrimination? Should they therefore abandon this useful indicator (albeit not a perfect one) of academic competence? If so, they may incur a cost in taking on some staff who turn out not to be fully competent.

Richard Epstein has pointed out that the 'burden of proof' issue is a special case of a general problem in statistical logic:

> In statistical language the entire thrust of the disparate impact rules is
> to minimise what statisticians call a Type II error – the chance that the

employer's illegal practice will be held to be legal. But any sensible legal system must also concern itself with Type I error – the chance that an employer will be found to have discriminated illegally when its conduct has been perfectly legal.[37]

Epstein points out that Type I errors bear a cost. Employers are forced to alter what they believe to be profit-maximising recruitment and selection procedures. As suggested in a later section, these costs do not fall entirely on employers and are likely to be passed on in various ways – for example, in a reduction in total recruitment or equilibrium wages.

Another way of conceptualising this issue is to think about anti-discrimination policies in the context of other types of legislation, for example that against pollution or in favour of safety standards. Veljanovski has pointed out that :

> the economic function of law is not to prevent all harm, but rather to balance the interests of the victim against the interests and welfare of the injurer and of consumers in general. In economic terms this means balancing the losses due to the harm and the costs of preventing the harm. When the sum of these costs is minimised we have the 'efficient' or 'optimal' level of harm ... Only rarely will economic considerations lead to such extreme solutions as the complete elimination of pollution or accidents, even if such radical solutions were technically feasible.[38]

The reversal of the burden of proof in discrimination cases is a choice to increase the level of enforcement of the law. It will result in greater compliance costs to employers and increase their chances of incurring compensation costs. These costs will in turn be passed on in various ways. Whether the marginal benefit to applicants will exceed the marginal cost to society as a whole has never been asked, let alone answered, as it is taken as axiomatic that the level of discrimination should be reduced.

37   R. Epstein, *Forbidden Grounds: The Case against Employment Discrimination Laws*, Harvard University Press, Cambridge, Mass., 1995, p. 223.

38   C. Veljanovski, *The Economics of Law*, Hobart Paper 114, Institute of Economic Affairs, 1990, p. 49.

against one sex. Now, as a result of a European Directive passed into UK law without debate in the Sex Discrimination (Indirect Discrimination and Burden of Proof) Regulations 2001, an employer has to prove innocence of discrimination. This reversal of a fundamental principle of English law has sent many employers into a funk. It implies that they must examine all their employment practices – advertisement, recruitment, training, promotion, pensions, dismissal – for any indication that men and women are treated differently, or even react differently. It appears that arguments about the importance to the business of a practice will carry little weight. It will require several years of cases before managers will really understand what these regulations mean. And to add to the confusion, the same shift in the burden of proof will take place in relation to race discrimination from 2003.

Another area that is causing increasing problems is allegations of employer-induced stress. The Disability Discrimination Act was not intended to cover stress. Indeed, it 'is worded in such a way that it clearly applies to physical disabilities', according to one expert. Yet Incomes Data Services report that already about one in five disability claims relate to 'depression, bad nerves, anxiety, mental illness, phobia, panic or other nervous disorders'.[39]

Stress is a phenomenon for which the medical basis is highly debatable, as Ruth Lea has recently argued.[40] Unlike visible disabilities, its symptoms are extraordinarily difficult for employers to recognise and evaluate. Referral to doctors is of little assistance.

39   N. MacErlean, 'The illness that dare not speak its name', *Observer*, 14 October 2001.

40   See R. Lea, *The 'Work–Life Balance' ... and all that: The re-regulation of the labour market*, Institute of Directors policy paper, April 2001. Ms Lea argues that while stress is certainly an important management issue, the 'medicalisation' of the problem is unhelpful to analysis or policy.

They are frequently unwilling to give an opinion and their judgement is unreliable: 'Employers hoping that a third party may spot a malingerer are always disappointed. Usually, medical reports will document any symptoms described by the patient and then simply repeat the employee's explanation of the causes.'[41]

Yet an employer's inability to recognise stress can be very costly: a manager of a Worcestershire County Council gypsy site was recently awarded £203,000 in compensation.[42]

Waiting down the road, too, is age discrimination legislation – which will in effect force employers to abandon fixed retirement ages. In order to prevent some workers continuing in employment way beyond their productive life, employers may have to devise tests of efficiency (which would certainly be challenged) or else expensively pay off people they wish to be rid of. This has already happened in the United States, where, for example, universities have had to pay large amounts of money to persuade elderly academics to retire and allow younger people to come through.[43]

The inherent problems of regulating in these areas are exacerbated by the way in which ministers allow poorly drafted or incomplete legislation to go through, allowing them subsequently to make ad hoc orders, and leaving employers facing considerable ambiguity. The 1997–date governments have been particularly guilty of this, possibly because they are trying to avoid upsetting employers' organisations on the one hand and trade unions on the other; it would inevitably upset someone if

41 A. Wetherfield, 'Take the stress out of work', *People Management*, 16 May 2002, p. 19.

42 P. Baty, 'The rising cost of blunders', *Sunday Times*, 4 November 2001.

43 For an analysis of the problems associated with age discrimination legislation, see R. A. Epstein, *Age Discrimination and Employment Law*, New Zealand Business Roundtable, 1999.

laws were clear and indisputable. Thus, in the Employment Bill currently going through Parliament, there is a vague requirement for employers to give 'proper consideration' to requests by female employees to work part time following return from maternity leave. It is predictable that, when such requests are turned down, there will be a series of tribunal applications seeking to prove that employers' consideration was not sufficiently proper. The DTI itself estimates that there could be 5,000 extra tribunal applications a year as a result of this provision.

Similarly, the bill is likely to create confusion over a proposed new right for women to know if male colleagues are being paid more than them for doing the same job. It is unclear what range of comparisons will be permitted, for Secretary of State Patricia Hewitt has admitted that this right clashes with employees' rights to privacy – which must also, of course, be taken into account by employers. If employees feel that insufficient comparative data have been revealed, they will be able to apply to a tribunal. Once again, employers will only gradually learn just how much information they are supposed to reveal.

To repeat, a major part of the problem is thus the continuing unpredictability and uncertainty of the law on employment rights. Such uncertainty falls particularly on smaller enterprises, for whom a wrong decision or interpretation of the law could turn out to be very expensive indeed. So long as uncertainty persists or intensifies we are likely to see continuing high levels of tribunal claims.

4 THE COSTS OF THE TRIBUNAL SYSTEM

We now move from explanations of the rise in applications to consideration of the costs associated with the employment tribunal system. This is a difficult and controversial task. We need to distinguish various different notions of cost.

Direct resource costs

Table 6 essays a rough estimate of the major costs of the operation of the system. The easiest element of costs to quantify is the resource costs directly associated with the running of the tribunal itself (the permanent staff, the lawyers and lay panellists, premises and expenses). These totalled £52 million in financial year 2000/01. To this we can certainly add a large part of the cost of running ACAS, probably around £30 million.

The significance of even these apparently straightforward costs is debatable, however, for we need as a 'counterfactual' the alternative regime which would exist in the absence of the tribunal system. Even if many aspects of labour market regulation were dropped, jurisdictions such as breach of contract and unlawful deduction from wages, for example, would presumably still exist. They would have to be dealt with through normal legal processes, which could well be more expensive than the tribunal system.

Table 6 **Some estimates of the resource costs of the tribunal system, 2000/01**

	Cost (£ million)
Employment Tribunals Service (a)	52
ACAS conciliation of individual disputes (b)	30
Management time and legal costs (c)	292
Extra recruitment costs (d)	341
Cost to applicants of bringing a case (e)	10
Other institutions' costs (f)	30
Employers' compliance costs (g)	250

Sources: (a) Employment Tribunals Service Annual Report and Accounts; (b) ACAS Annual Report, own estimate of proportion of costs; (c) and (d) CBI estimate; (e) grossing, updating and uprating figures from N. Tremlett and N. Banerji, *The 1992 Survey of Industrial Tribunal Applications*, Employment Department Research Series 22, 1994; (f) own estimate, see text; (g) see below.

Once we move outside the formal institutional set-up, costs attributable to tribunals immediately become more contentious. According to the DTI,[1] costs to employers include legal expenses and the cost of management time. Where firms hire outside legal assistance, these costs are reasonably objective; where in-house legal expertise is employed costs are more difficult to evaluate. So is management time. According to a survey of tribunal cases in 1996/97, senior managers spent a median 16 hours on all tribunal applications (27 hours on those that went to a hearing). All legal and management costs together were estimated to have been £2,000 per application in 1996. Updated for inflation, these average costs would produce a total figure for all applications of just over £290 million in 2000/01. These figures may be contestable, but they do not seem to be wildly controversial.

---

1   Department of Trade and Industry, *Routes to Resolution: Improving Dispute Resolution in Britain*, July 2001.

More tenuously, the DTI argues that costs attributable to the tribunal system include the cost of recruiting replacement employees if the complainant resigns or is dismissed. The average cost of recruiting a new employee is put at £3,500. The Confederation of British Industry (CBI) reckons new recruitment to be necessary in 75 per cent of cases, and this therefore adds an extra £340 million, to give a CBI estimate of total employer costs of just over £630 million[2] in 2000/01. There are reasons to query the relevance of this estimate. If there were no government regulation and tribunals, unsatisfactory employees would still have to be replaced, and costs would be incurred. About 60,000 tribunal applicants in 2000/01 were claiming unfair dismissal and had therefore left employment. If they had no legal protection most of them would have to be replaced anyway (indeed, we would probably expect dismissals to increase), so it is unclear why the CBI considers their replacement to be a cost imposed by the tribunal system.

Next, not to be forgotten, are the costs to individuals of bringing claims. Some official estimates were made in the early 1990s, and uprating them for inflation and the increased number of applications gives a figure of £10 million. Again the calculation of this figure could be queried in detail, but it does not seem implausible; the measurable financial costs of taking an application to tribunal are modest.

Other resource costs are incurred by various bodies that support tribunal applications. These include trade unions, Citizens Advice Bureaux, the Commission for Racial Equality, the

---

2   CBI press release, 21 August 2001, and telephone conversation with CBI researcher.

Equal Opportunities Commission, the Disability Rights Commission, and various charities. There are no published estimates of the total amount spent by these organisations (which engage in a variety of other activities) in supporting tribunal applications, but it is unlikely to be less than £30 million per year.[3] However, many of these costs would be incurred even in the absence of the tribunal system if the alternative was civil action through the courts.

Compensation

Note that these figures do not include the compensation that employers have to pay as a result of tribunal decisions – according to official figures, around £25 million in 2000/01 – plus compensation paid in pre-tribunal settlements. This latter figure is unknown, but on plausible assumptions is probably a further £20 million or so.[4] Compensation payments should not be treated analytically in the same way as resource costs, as they are a form of transfer payment like social security benefits or gifts. Although they clearly have significance from the point of view of the parties involved, and the incentives they create, they do not represent a direct use of productive resources.

---

3   Unions alone must account for a substantial proportion of this. A TUC survey (in TUC, *Focus on Employment* Tribunals, February 2001) showed that in 1999/2000 respondent unions that collated data recorded supporting 6,478 tribunal claims. The total supported by all unions is likely to have been at least twice that in 2000/01. If average costs of officials' time and legal costs were around £1,000 per case on average (i.e. about £1,200 less than employers spent), this would amount to around £15 million.

4   A large proportion of the 45 per cent of applications that are settled outside tribunals are likely to have resulted in some compensation being paid. However, it is known that settlements prior to a hearing are substantially less on average than those awarded by a tribunal.

Compliance costs

In addition to the costs that employers incur in tribunal cases, there are also the very substantial costs associated with measures they take in order to avoid being in breach of employment law. The DTI refers approvingly to firms that have formal disputes procedures, pointing out that

> Employers with written procedures are more likely to reach a settlement or have an application against them withdrawn than employers without written procedures. At hearing, employers with procedures are far more likely to defend a case successfully than those who do not.[5]

However, such benefits are not costless. To devise, implement and monitor even the simplest of such procedures takes valuable management time. In large organisations specialist personnel departments devote substantial resources to ensuring compliance with equal opportunity and other labour market regulation. Awareness of company disciplinary procedures and anti-discrimination policies is something which all employees in such firms have to be made aware of through off-the-job training and staff development programmes unknown to previous generations. Adherence to central and local government policies in these areas is one of the main reasons why public sector employees spend more time in off-the-job training activities than private sector employees. Smaller firms are, of course, less able to afford the time and other resources for such work.

Employers who do not have formal procedures in place have

---

5   DTI, op. cit., p. 3.

been routinely penalised as tribunals take this into account when setting the level of awards. While it is understandable that tribunals should have tried to use the existence or non-existence of internal procedures as a guide to the degree of culpability involved, there is something questionable about a system that has in effect 'fined' smaller firms for not having procedures which they were not legally obliged to institute. As we shall see, the new Employment Bill is intended to strengthen the legal backing for this practice. In the Regulatory Impact Assessment[6] for the proposal to require all firms to possess basic formal disciplinary and grievance procedures, the cost to employers currently without such procedures is put at between £46 and £86 million (set-up costs) plus recurrent annual costs of management time at £42–90 million. Around 20 per cent of the workforce appears currently to work in organisations with no grievance or disciplinary procedure. If the other 80 per cent are in organisations that incur costs similar to those projected in the DTI's figures, this would imply that between £168 and £360 million of management time is already being spent annually on running these procedures alone – say a central estimate of £250 million.

This expenditure (surely only the tip of the iceberg, given the size of the personnel function in large organisations) could be regarded as a minimum level of compliance costs necessary to reduce the chances of adverse tribunal judgments. And it simply covers procedures, not the substantive cost of implementing specific employment regulations, which is vastly higher.[7]

---

6 See DTI website.

7 For example, according to the CBI, the working time directive alone costs employers £7.65 billion. See M. Gove, 'Brown waves farewell to social democracy', *The Times*, 16 July 2002.

Table 7 Indirect costs incurred by employers in tribunal cases

	Unfair dismissal	Breach of contract	Wages Act	Sex/race discrimination	Redundancy payments
Increased staff stress	14%	13%	12%	27%	8%
Adverse reputation as an employer	7%	6%	9%	12%	2%
Damaged workplace relations	5%	6%	5%	15%	0%
Lower output	3%	5%	5%	9%	1%

Source: Department of Trade and Industry, *Routes to Resolution: Improving Dispute Resolution in Britain,* July 2001.

Indirect costs

Employers often complain that the overt financial costs incurred as a result of the tribunal system are less significant than the indirect costs in the form of stress on staff, damage to the employer's reputation, worsened workplace relations and lower output. Table 7, based on responses to a DTI survey, shows that such costs are widely experienced.

This table shows the proportion of respondents who claimed to have incurred various less quantifiable costs as a result of tribunal cases. There is a considerable variation between jurisdictions. Employers perceived sex and race discrimination cases to be those that produced the greatest indirect costs. These areas are also, as we saw earlier, those where compensation payments are the highest. Median awards in 2000/01 were £5,499 in sexual and £8,012 in racial discrimination cases as against only £2,744 in unfair dismissal cases.

The fear of damage to a firm's reputation is a main reason why so many employers, as we have seen, settle claims in advance of tribunal hearings. Tribunals are open to the public, and colourful allegations against employers are a staple fare of newspapers.

Applicants know that they possess a considerable weapon, particularly against large firms which rely on their public image for marketing purposes. Many must also be aware that two significant findings of racial discrimination against an employer can lead to a detailed and potentially costly investigation of its practices by the Commission for Racial Equality.

It should not be forgotten in all this, however, that applicants can also bear substantial indirect costs as a result of tribunal applications. A decision to go to a tribunal is often a difficult one for a conscientious applicant. There is considerable stress involved in pursuing a claim: 17 per cent of those who withdraw their applications prior to reaching a tribunal hearing do so because they feel there is too much stress involved in continuing. It is known that almost half of those pursuing a claim end up in a lower-status job after taking an employer to a tribunal; more than a third claim their employment prospects have been damaged, and a quarter experience a spell of unemployment.

This qualification is certainly necessary to the view that tribunal applicants are malicious troublemakers. One issue may be whether some tribunal jurisdictions that put the onus on individuals to seek redress might possibly be better served by an inspection regime, as is the case with health and safety and used to be the case with the Wages Councils. This is an issue to which we will return.

There have not been any attempts to put a monetary value on these indirect costs, although in principle it could be attempted. They are clearly likely to be substantial.

Emphasis on costs misleads

What should count as a cost, therefore, is a problem. Firms naturally focus on the costs they experience as a result of tribunal applications against them, but such an approach can divert attention from more fundamental issues. Arguably the really important objections to employment tribunals are those relating to the underlying interventions in labour markets which give rise to tribunal jurisdictions. Even in a world with 100 per cent compliance and no tribunal applications, many forms of labour market intervention would impose substantial costs on the economy in general, rather than simply on the parties apparently directly concerned.

5 THE WIDER COSTS OF LABOUR MARKET REGULATION

The Better Regulation Task Force has concluded that 'not enough is known within Government of the true impact of employment regulations'.[1] This is certainly true. One difficulty is that much discussion of the costs of labour market regulation perpetuates the fallacy that the main losers from excessive regulation are employers and shareholders. The fallacy arises from the assumption that there are no further consequences other than the immediate cost to the parties involved.

Labour market regulation as a 'stealth tax'

One way to analyse the impact of a wide variety of labour market regulation is to recognise that it acts as a form of taxation on employers. American labour economists Richard Vedder and Lowell Galloway[2] saw it as a form of 'stealth taxation' before that term became common in a different context. The important point to note is that, like other forms of tax ostensibly paid by employers (such as value added tax or national insurance contributions), the burden is not ultimately borne by the employer, but is passed on.

---

1   Better Regulation Task Force, *Employment Regulation: Striking a balance*, May 2002, p. 20.

2   R. Vedder and L. Galloway, Laws, Litigation and Labor Markets: Some New Evidence, Pacific Research Institute website www.pacificresearch.org September 1995.

Figure 3   **Impact of a mandated worker benefit**

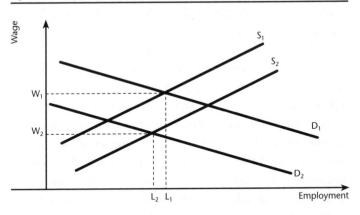

In the diagram,[3] the initial supply and demand curves for labour are shown as S_1 and D_1 respectively. Equilibrium wage is W_1, and equilibrium employment L_1. Suppose a new labour market benefit is mandated for employees, for example the introduction of parental leave, paid holidays, or an employer-provided pension. This is equivalent to a tax per unit of labour employed, and this is shown by a shift of the demand curve for labour to D_2 (the vertical distance between the old and new demand curves being the unit cost to the employer of providing the benefit).

If the benefit provided by the employer is valued by the employee, it will have a monetary equivalent – the amount by which

3   A variant of diagrams used by, amongst others, Charles Baird, *Unjustifiable dismissal – the economics of an unjust employment tax*, Free Market Foundation of Southern Africa Monograph 19, 1998, and J. T. Addison and W. S. Siebert, *Regulating European Labour Markets: More costs than benefits?*, Hobart Paper 138, Institute of Economic Affairs, 1999.

the wage rate would need to be increased to give the same increase in utility. The supply curve will therefore shift from S_1 to S_2, the vertical distance between the curves being the monetary equivalent value to a worker of the new benefit.

As a consequence of the shifts of the demand and supply curves, a new equilibrium wage (W_2) and employment level (L_2) will be determined. In the diagram, *the wage and the level of employment fall.* Is this an inevitable outcome of the introduction of mandated benefit? Manipulation of the diagram shows that the wage must fall if the benefit has a positive cost to the employer and some positive value, however small, to the employee.[4] These seem highly plausible assumptions. What happens to employment is, however, debatable – for it depends on the relative size of the shifts of the curves. If both curves shift by exactly the same amount – in other words, the employees place the same monetary value on the benefit as it costs the employer to provide – employment is unchanged even though the wage falls (in fact it would fall by the full extent of the 'tax'). If employees value the benefit more than it costs the employer to provide, employment would actually increase – but the result would be a fall in the wage by an amount greater than the cost incurred by the employer!

However, it seems more plausible to assume that the benefit will be valued less than the cost the employer incurs to provide it.[5] Some employees at least would prefer a higher wage to, for ex-

---

4   Looking at it differently, the percentage of the 'tax' which is passed on to employees in the form of reduced wages depends on the values of the elasticities of demand for and supply of labour. For a proof, see Baird, op. cit., pp. 57–60. For an empirical estimate of the proportion of the costs of employment protection passed on in California, see Vedder and Galloway, op. cit.

5   Baird argues that this follows from an analogy with Coase's Theorem. In a famous article (R. H. Coase, 'The Problem of Social Cost', *Journal of Law and Economics*,

ample, an employer-provided pension. Administering a pension scheme is anyway likely to incur resource costs to the employer which are not reflected in benefits to the employee. Similarly the employer who gives parental leave will incur costs in recruiting and training substitute workers over and above the salary paid for a replacement employee.

The analysis suggests, therefore, that employees as a group bear the cost of labour market regulation (and, by extension, the cost of tribunal compensation) by a combination of falling wages and falling employment. This may not be how it appears to the non-economist, but this is a most important insight, as much of the support for labour market regulation comes from the belief that the employer should 'pay' for mandated benefits. Much rhetoric from business organisations unfortunately tends to perpetuate this misunderstanding, and enables proponents of regulation to paint critics as apologists for business interests.

The distributional impact

The direct impact of any new regulation will fall unequally. Firms with more women employees, for example, will be more affected by parental leave provisions than others. Firms with more unionised workers will be more directly affected by legislation granting recognition rights.

More generally, we could add that mandates and other

October 1960, pp. 1–44) Ronald Coase argued that, in a free market with no transactions costs, property rights would end up in the possession of those who valued them most highly. By analogy, people would have negotiated the right to a paid holiday (say) if they valued it more highly than it cost the employer to provide it.

regulations have a rather subtler distributional effect within the workforce. They generally tend to protect 'insiders' (established workers) against 'outsiders' (young people, immigrants, women returners). Furthermore, continuing the analogy between regulation and taxation, just as over time tax revenue may be undermined by evasion and avoidance, so we may expect employers, shareholders and other investors to alter their behaviour as they understand the regulatory environment better. Firms will try to avoid the impact of regulation by, for instance, recruiting less from groups likely to make significant use of mandated benefits such as parental leave. They will switch resources to areas that are not so highly regulated, for example by moving production abroad, or make greater use of self-employed contractors. The result may be slower economic growth, but no permanent decline in the rate of return to shareholders.

Consider three areas of intervention as examples: equal pay and discrimination; employment protection and unlawful dismissal; and working time regulations.

Equal pay and discrimination

Economic analysis of employer discrimination points out that 'pure' discrimination involves preferring one group to another on non-economic grounds, that is on a basis other than the marginal productivity of individuals. Logically this is costly for employers, who will be paying more for labour than they need to. However, if employers differ in their taste for discrimination, with some being more open minded, those who discriminate less will gain a cost advantage. In competitive markets where all are free to enter, the argument is that discrimination should in the long run be self-correcting.[6] According to this view the persistence of discrimination over long periods of time tends to occur only where competition is restricted, probably by the state. Thus discrimination in apartheid South Africa or the pre-1960s American South could be maintained only by legal backing that effectively criminalised firms employing integrated workforces.[7]

A more subtle analysis of discrimination was developed in the 1970s from the work of Arrow and Phelps.[8] This approach saw employer discrimination, not as costly self-indulgence on the part of bigoted employers, but as a cost-minimising strategy in the face of information problems. Thus employers, faced with large numbers of unknown applicants, took refuge in stereotypes based on real or imagined statistical regularities such as 'women don't stay with the firm long'. Discrimination on this basis is unfair to those who do not fit the stereotype. It was argued, however, that it was likely to be persistent as it was based on what was believed to be profit-maximising behaviour. This persistence was argued to justify government intervention.

Again, however, it could be argued that competition might encourage employers to search for more information about

---

6   An argument first developed in G. Becker, *The Economics of Discrimination*, Chicago University Press, Chicago, Ill., 1957.

7   R. Epstein, *Forbidden Grounds: The Case against Discrimination Laws*, Harvard University Press, Cambridge, Mass., 1995. Epstein points out that there was a big gain in the relative pay of black workers as the so-called 'Jim Crow' laws, protecting white jobs in the American South, were dismantled. The gains in relative pay since then, despite ever wider definitions of discrimination and the ruling out of any form of 'disparate treatment', however indirect, have been modest.

8   K. Arrow, 'Some mathematical models of race in the labor market', in A. Pascal (ed.), *Racial discrimination in economic life*, Lexington Books, Lexington, Mass., 1972, pp. 83–102; E. Phelps, 'The statistical theory of racism and sexism', *American Economic Review*, 62, 1972, pp. 659–61.

individual applicants rather than relying on stereotypes. It is also possible that, in the absence of regulations to forbid it, potential employees who did not conform to the stereotype could signal this to employers by, for instance, working trial periods at lower rates of pay.

Whatever the analysis of their causes, explicit racial and sexual discrimination in employment, and the payment of different wages to men and women on grounds of gender alone, have been outlawed for many years. The expanding case load of tribunals reflects the way in which new legislation and court and tribunal judgments have expanded the concept of discrimination to embrace all sorts of indirect disadvantage that some groups may suffer, and have expanded definitions of pay to cover all aspects of conditions and rewards associated with employment, such as pensions, holidays and promotions.

Fear of falling foul of ever-changing interpretations of the law can lead employers to over-compensate by paying groups with differing levels of productivity the same wage. This raises costs and in the long run may create unemployment. Those in work may gain, but those out of work (likely to be the most disadvantaged groups) find it difficult to get jobs as they cannot price themselves into employment by offering to work at lower pay. Recourse to tribunals, and consequent compensation, are open mainly to those who are already on the inside as employees.

Working time regulations

The EU Working Time Directive, which the UK has adopted, limits working hours per week and mandates minimum rest periods, maximum lengths of night shifts and minimum holidays. This imposes extra costs on businesses. The rationale is the belief that in a free market employers will coerce workers into long hours which will damage health and family life.

The empirical basis for this claim is shaky, for the evidence is that long hours are in the main voluntary. Among those working the longest hours are professional and highly skilled workers who are strongly committed to their careers. The UK is often assumed to be exceptionally prone to a 'long hours culture', notwithstanding the fact that our average hours worked fell by 3 per cent over the last decade and are anyway considerably below those found in the USA, Japan, Canada, Australia and New Zealand.[9] Nor do our working hours, admittedly longer than those of some European neighbours, prove particularly damaging to health – at least as far as this is manifested in injury rates at work. The UK has the lowest fatality rate at work in the European Union and its accident rate is less than half the EU average.

Arguments for regulating working time are built on the implicit assumption that everybody has similar preferences as regards work and leisure. But this is not the case: attitudes to work and need for extra money, for example, differ throughout the population. Those who would prefer to work longer hours, either because they prefer extra money to extra hours watching TV or because they are absorbed in their work, are prevented from doing so by restrictions on working time. Although much is made of the alleged need for 'Work–Life Balance',[10] regulation of working hours means in practice a paternalistic imposition of a particular view of how time should be spent. It does not fully take into account, for

9   *OECD Employment Outlook*, various years.
10 See R. Lea, *The 'Work–Life Balance'… and all that: The re-regulation of the labour market*, Institute of Directors policy paper, April 2001.

example, the way in which preferred hours vary over the life cycle in response to family and other commitments: at certain times, people *want* to work more, to bring in more income or to enhance their future promotion prospects.

Moreover, the degree to which working hours regulation can be enforced differs through the population. Its impact is much greater on production workers, for example, than on professionals. Employees in the latter group have an element of their working time predetermined, but otherwise decide for themselves how much 'partly unmeasured working time'[11] they spend on their careers. And there are variations in the ability of different occupations to engage in 'moonlighting' – working for more than one employer as a means of evading limits on hours worked.

Employment protection/unlawful dismissal

Employment protection legislation makes it more difficult to fire workers. Firms have to go through formal procedures and pay compensation. If they do not, they are liable to be taken before a tribunal. More has been written by economists on this topic than on most other types of labour market regulation.

Early discussions of the effects of job protection tended to emphasise the way in which it reallocated unemployment over the business cycle. If it is made more expensive to fire workers, employers will hold on to them longer in a downturn. However, they

---

11 An official guide points out that the specific characteristics of this activity 'are such that, without being required to do so by the employer, the worker may also do [additional] work which is not measured or pre-determined or can be determined by the worker himself'. Department of Trade and Industry, *Your guide to the working time regulations*, March 2000, p. 20.

will also be slower to rehire in an upturn, for fear that the recovery may be reversed and they will have to incur firing costs. According to this view the average unemployment level over the cycle is little affected (although there will be distributional effects with insiders gaining at the expense of outsiders). However, more recent hysteresis[12] models suggest that anything that delays rehiring may contribute to permanently higher unemployment as workers' skills decay and their commitment to work is undermined. The difference in job protection between the USA and major European economies in the 1990s was often cited as one of the reasons for the much lower rate of long-term unemployment in the USA.

Sophisticated attempts to test this proposition began with Lazear's cross-country study of the impact of severance pay on employment.[13] Using aggregate data for 20 countries from 1956 to 1984, Lazear found that dismissal pay was negatively related to the employment–population ratio, labour force participation and hours worked, and positively associated with the unemployment rate.

As is the way with pioneering work of this kind, later authors were critical and proposed using alternative indicators of employment protection, different statistical specifications and different datasets. More than a decade of such macroeconomic studies is surveyed by Addison and Teixeira,[14] who conclude that, although

---

12 'Hysteresis' in this context denotes the tendency of the natural rate of unemployment (or NAIRU) to match the actual rate. It is an extreme case of unemployment 'persistence': see G. Alogoskoufis and A. Manning, 'Unemployment persistence', *Economic Policy*, 7, 1988, pp. 427–69.

13 E. P. Lazear, 'Job Security Provisions and Employment', *Quarterly Journal of Economics*, 105, October 1990, pp. 699–726.

14 J. T. Addison and P. Teixeira, 'The Economics of Employment Protection', unpublished manuscript, 2001.

there remain some notable dissenting voices, most analysts now agree that employment protection legislation does have a negative effect on employment. However, the impact is not on prime-age male workers, but on women and young workers.[15]

Apart from the studies on the aggregate impact of job protection, there have also been some very interesting microeconomic studies using firm-level data to support the same general conclusion. For example, Siebert and Morton use personnel records to contrast plants in UK subsidiaries of five multinationals with matched plants in other EU countries.[16] They find that plants in the UK tend to employ a wider range of staff and include relatively more of those with less experience and shorter job tenure – and relatively fewer prime-age workers – than those in countries with much tighter employment protection rules.

These and other interventions in the labour market, then, raise costs to employers and tend to reduce employment. But an important point to note from all three of the examples briefly discussed here is that the impact of regulation does not fall equally on different groups of workers. Some gain and some lose. This is relevant to the question of who makes applications to employment tribunals, the question to which we next turn.

15 See T. Slinger, 'Some labour market implications of employment legislation', *Labour Market Trends*, September 2001, pp. 445–54.

16 J. Morton and S. Siebert, 'Labour Market Regimes and Worker Recruitment and Retention in the European Union: Plant Comparisons', *British Journal of Industrial Relations*, 39, 4 December 2001, pp. 505–28.

6 WHO APPLIES TO TRIBUNALS?

Relatively little research has been done to analyse who applicants are, and what sort of factors influence them to make applications. Analysis of the 1992 Survey of Industrial Tribunal Applications[1] indicated that two-thirds of applicants were male and one-third female; 90 per cent were white. By the time of the 1998 survey, the proportion of females had risen to 40 per cent, although surprisingly the proportion of applicants from ethnic minorities actually fell to 7 per cent.

The 1998 survey provides information on other characteristics of applicants, for example age. The average applicant in this survey was in his or her early forties, although redundancy payment applicants were older (with 45 per cent aged over 50). Wages Act and discrimination applicants, however, tended to be younger, on average in their mid-thirties.

Two-thirds of applicants were married or living as married, but those bringing redundancy payment cases were more likely to be widowed, divorced or separated than other applicants. One interesting finding was that 5 per cent of applicants had previously made a tribunal application. It is known that there is a very small number of applicants who have made several applications to

---

1   N. Tremlett and N. Banerji, *The 1992 Survey of Industrial Tribunal Applications*, Employment Department Research Series 22, February 1994.

Table 8 **Tribunal applications by size of workplace (column percentages)**

	All jurisdictions	Unfair dismissal	Breach of contract	Pay deductions	Discrimination	Redundancy payments
Fewer than 10 employees	29	24	36	37	14	48
10–24	22	20	23	29	25	12
25–99	25	26	24	19	25	29
100–199	10	12	8	5	16	1
200–999	9	10	8	7	9	5
1,000+	6	7	2	3	11	5

Source: Department of Trade and Industry, *Routes to Resolution: Improving Dispute Resolution in Britain*, op. cit.

tribunals over the years.[2]

In trying to determine who applies, we need to bear in mind that there are individual characteristics and firm or workplace characteristics that interact. Table 8 illustrates this.

The table shows two things. First, applicants to tribunals come disproportionately from smaller workplaces. It has been pointed out already that such workplaces are less likely to have formal grievance and disciplinary procedures, meaning that issues which might in larger organisations be dealt with internally instead turn into tribunal applications. However, this explanation needs the qualification that only a small minority of firms have no grievance procedure whatsoever, and the existence of such proce-

2   Department of Trade and Industry, *Findings from the 1998 Survey of Employment Tribunal Applications*, DTI Employment Relations Research Series 13, 2002. Some 'serial applicants' have run up many cases. One particularly busy complainant has a fifteen-year history of cases against, *inter alia*, the BBC, Enfield Council, Enfield Racial Equality Council, Brent Council and Hackney Council. Her most recent claim threatened to bankrupt a voluntary agency, Hackney Action for Racial Equality. See Michael Seamark, 'In 15 years of complaining, this woman has cost taxpayers £170,000', *Daily Mail*, 27 March 2002.

dures within a firm has not prevented large numbers of employees ignoring them and proceeding directly to a tribunal application. One problem is that in the smallest firms there can be little or no separation between the owner or manager adjudicating on grievances and the person about whom a complaint is made.

Second, there are considerable variations between the workplace size distribution when we disaggregate the different types of application. As the table shows, almost half of redundancy payment applications come from employees in very small workplaces with less than ten employees – although only 18 per cent of all employees are in workplaces of this scale. Large employers are much more likely to pay the statutory amounts of redundancy pay than smaller employers, probably because they have greater financial resources and are more likely to be fully aware of their obligations. Large firms' personnel departments have a professional responsibility to be fully briefed on these matters. However, the pattern is rather different for applications concerning discrimination. Only 14 per cent of all applications under this jurisdiction concern workplaces with less than 10 employees.

Discrimination applications

The relatively greater proportion of discrimination applicants drawn from larger workplaces appears on the face of it rather surprising, for larger firms are much more likely to have formal equal opportunities policies. Possibly these act to raise expectations among women, ethnic minorities and those with disabilities, and thus may lead to applications when firms seem to fall short of the standards they set. More cynically, applicants will be aware that a large firm with a national or even international market is more likely to settle a claim quickly rather than proceed to tribunal in the face of potential damage to its reputation. And, of course, larger firms are perceived to have a greater ability to pay.

Another likely factor here is that very small firms in particular may tend to have a more homogeneous workforce, with employees drawn from particular ethnic groups, or predominantly from one gender, and thus discrimination issues do not arise with the same frequency as they do in larger firms with more diverse workforces.[3]

A striking finding from analysis of the 1998 Workforce Employment Relations Survey is that workplace grievances and tribunal applications concerning discrimination do not appear to be closely linked to the scale of pay disadvantage suffered by types of complainant. The rate of complaint appears if anything to increase the higher the firm's pay in relation to its competitors.

As one analyst, Stephen Pudney,[4] has pointed out, resort to grievance procedures and tribunal applications over discrimination issues may be more common among the more educated and able of the workforce. The 1998 Survey of Employment Tribunal Applications shows that 71 per cent of all discrimination applicants are in non-manual occupations, as against only 57 per cent for all tribunal applications. They are more likely to be members of unions or staff associations (38 per cent compared with 22 per cent of all applicants).

---

3   It must also be noted that firms employing fewer than fifteen people are currently exempt from disability discrimination legislation, though this exemption will end by 2004.

4   S. Pudney, 'Pay Differentials, Discrimination and Worker Grievances', paper presented at the Royal Economic Society annual conference, Durham, April 2001.

Discrimination applicants also earn more on average than applicants as a whole. Certainly the more highly paid are, other things being equal, likely to get higher compensation – the City analyst mentioned in Chapter 1 is an example. Her success in winning a record pay-out has led to a number of similar claims from highly paid female City employees, the latest of which is said to be seeking £4 million compensation for her forced resignation.[5]

This leads Pudney to suggest that low-skilled and poorly paid employees are those who are least likely to be helped by the tribunal system, and he goes on to argue that tribunals may thus be relatively ineffective as an anti-discrimination device.

Pudney also finds that discrimination applications appear to be more common among public sector employees than those in the private sector, when other factors are controlled for. This is another apparently perverse finding, given the importance attached to this issue in some government departments and local authorities. In some parts of the public sector there is arguably a highly developed grievance and litigation culture which rule-based organisations like local government and the civil service tend to encourage, although it is also asserted by some commentators that the poor quality of management in the public sector is a factor.[6]

Be that as it may, a similar pattern of over-representation of tribunal applicants among the voluntary sector is also suggestive. Not-for-profit organisations as a whole account for 10 per cent of all discrimination applications.[7] Charities are twice as likely as

5   'Sexist directors forced me from the company I created', *Daily Telegraph*, 10 July 2002.
6   Professor Roger Seifert of the University of Keele, quoted in P. Baty, 'The rising cost of blunders', *Sunday Times*, 4 November 2001.
7   DTI, op. cit., p. 17.

other employers to face a tribunal application.[8] And the largest single pay-out for a race discrimination case has not been against a commercial company but rather against the British Medical Association.[9]

Another noteworthy finding from the 1998 Survey of Employment Tribunal Applications is that black workers are considerably more likely than South Asian workers to be applicants in discrimination cases. Black workers accounted for 16 per cent of all race and sex discrimination cases compared with 14 per cent from South Asian backgrounds, although the latter group considerably outnumber the former in the workforce as a whole – with Pakistani and Bangladeshi workers being the poorest-paid ethnic groupings.

To find that discrimination applications are more common among relatively well-paid, educated people working in large firms, government or charities is very interesting, as is the fact that some ethnic groups are under-represented amongst applicants. These findings echo the evidence from other areas that many government interventions in the labour market are not particularly well targeted in relation to their ostensible objectives.

Unfair dismissal applications

Other writers have used the 1998 Workplace Employment Relations Survey to analyse the determinants of what still remains the largest single category of applications, unfair dismissal. As we have seen, there is a strong cyclical component in the level of un-

8   P. McCurry, 'Wronged rights', *Guardian*, 1 August 2001.
9   'Record payout for Asian surgeon', BBC Business News website, 21 June 2002.

fair dismissal applications. But at any one time there is considerable variation in the incidence of applications between employers and between different groups of employees.

In a three-stage analysis, Knight and Latreille[10] looked at the determinants of disciplinary sanctions against workers, dismissal rates and tribunal applications; workers who are disciplined are more likely to be dismissed and therefore end up claiming unlawful dismissal.

They show that disciplinary action and dismissals are more likely for *males* than for females, for *full-time* than for part-time employees, for *manual* workers than for those in white-collar jobs, for *younger* workers rather than for older workers, and for people from *ethnic minorities* rather than for whites. Subsequent tribunal applications are more likely from those in large workplaces. Again, there are occupational variations, with a dismissed manual worker being more likely to apply, and with ethnic minority workers also being associated with a high rate of application.

Another finding that is worth noting is that 'dismissal and disciplinary sanction rates are lower when unions have a more significant presence'.[11] This is likely to lead to fewer tribunal applications. This might be considered to be another aspect of the downside of the union reforms of the 1980s and 1990s. If unions were stronger, there might be fewer tribunal applications. Advocates of unions, such as the Oxford School writers of the 1960s or more recently the influential American writers Robert Freeman and James Medoff, have seen some positive benefits from union

---

10   K. G. Knight and P. L. Latreille, 'Discipline, Dismissals and Complaints to Employment Tribunals', *British Journal of Industrial Relations*, 38, 4 December 2000, pp. 533–55.

11   Ibid, p. 49.

membership. Freeman and Medoff[12] famously spoke of 'two faces of unionism': against the negative, monopoly side may be counterposed a more positive side where union members display lower turnover than non-union members. Possibly the collective 'voice' provided by unionism reduces the need for 'exit' by dissatisfied workers – and with it recourse to tribunals. On the other hand, unions may be using their influence to force on firms a higher level of compliance than they would choose or is strictly required. The question needs further investigation.

Finally, a case of the dog that didn't bark: Knight and Latreille attempted to test the hypothesis that employees in workplaces where good human resource management practices were followed would be less likely to make tribunal applications for unfair dismissal. Interestingly, they were unable to support the hypothesis. The existence of formal discipline and dismissal procedures did not reduce the probability that tribunal applications would be made *when other factors were controlled for*. This suggests that the high incidence of tribunal claims among smaller firms may not be the result simply of inadequate procedures but the consequence of other factors such as the vulnerability of these firms to cyclical downturns, the type of work undertaken and the characteristics of the workforce.

The authors were also unable to find a relationship between applications and indicators of various 'high commitment management workplace practices' such as quality circles, briefing groups, joint consultative committees, share ownership, profit-related schemes and training in supervisory skills. The only such practice

12 R. B. Freeman and J. L. Medoff, *What Do Unions Do?*, Basic Books, New York, 1984.

that did significantly affect claims was the provision of financial information – which had the perverse effect of *increasing* the probability of a tribunal application.

This section has pointed out that, although not enough is yet known about tribunal applicants, what we do know suggests that they are far from being a 'random draw' from the employed population. They are drawn disproportionately from smaller firms, but for discrimination cases those in larger firms, the public sector and charities are over-represented. There is a strong suggestion that certain types of individuals are more likely to take advantage of employment tribunals, with the corollary that other groups are less willing, or less able, to benefit from the system. This is an important insight, which does not yet seem to have penetrated policy thinking.

7 REFORMING THE TRIBUNAL SYSTEM

We have seen that the increase in tribunal applications is costly for firms and the government, for applicants themselves and for other workers who might wish to obtain employment on terms other than those enforced by the tribunal system. We have also seen in the previous chapter that there may be reasons to suppose that the tribunal system is not a particularly effective means of helping the most vulnerable members of the workforce. In this section we turn to considering planned and possible reforms of the employment tribunal system.

Tribunal ownership

One issue that has surfaced recently is a Whitehall turf war about who should control tribunals. In August 2001, following a review by Sir Andrew Leggatt of the work of all types of tribunals in the UK, the Lord Chancellor proposed that his department take over 'ownership' of the tribunal system as a whole. There are currently 70 different types of tribunal in the UK, covering such varied fields as tax, social security and immigration. At the moment, they are controlled by the sponsoring department, which in the case of employment tribunals is the DTI, and have their own methods of recruitment, processes, procedures and reporting mechanisms.

Sir Andrew's argument – echoed by Lord Irvine – is that tribunals may be perceived as lacking independence, as they are ultimately controlled by a minister who appoints the personnel involved: 'The tribunal neither appears to be independent, nor is it independent in fact. Responsibility for tribunals and their administration should not lie with those whose policies or decisions it is the tribunals' duty to consider.'[1]

There is some attraction to the idea of having a standard set of procedures, for instance in appointing tribunal members to bodies that are ultimately part of a common legal framework. Sir Andrew also makes encouraging noises in his report about the need to cut back on the use of solicitors and barristers, and to restore the tribunal system to something like the original informality envisaged at the time of its creation. However, the proposal has not been widely acclaimed. The TUC believes, despite Sir Andrew's remarks, that takeover by the Lord Chancellor's office would increase, rather than decrease, the formality and 'legalism' of the tribunal process. Lawyers, on the other hand, insist that their services are increasingly necessary. As one employment lawyer puts it, 'employment litigation is becoming a much more difficult area of the law and it is too complicated for people to represent themselves'.[2]

Although the proposal may make sense as part of some other agenda for tidying up government, it would be unlikely to address significantly the problems to which critics of employment tribunals have drawn attention. Removing responsibility

1 *Tribunals for Users: One System, One Service*, report of the Review of Tribunals by Sir Andrew Leggatt, March 2001, p. 2. This is the argument that surfaced in relation to employment tribunals in the case of *Smith v. Secretary of State for Trade and Industry*.

2 Quoted in H. MacDonnell, 'Tribunals in turmoil', *Daily Mail*, 15 January 2001.

for employment tribunals from the department responsible for developing employment legislation does not seem to be an obvious way of improving the way in which employment is regulated.

Some of the issues discussed by Sir Andrew should have been picked up by the Employment Tribunal System Taskforce set up in November 2001. This has not yet, at the time of writing, reported.

Alternative dispute resolution

The costs and delays involved in tribunal hearings have led to interest in alternative forms of dispute resolution.[3] Proposals for such schemes date back to the early 1980s and may take a variety of forms, involving principles of *mediation* (an impartial third party steering the complainant and the respondent towards an agreement) or *conciliation* (similar, but with the third party taking a more proactive role) or *arbitration* (where the third party hears both sides of the argument and delivers a binding judgment). Such processes can involve greater or lesser degrees of formality.

The third party involved can in principle be a range of agencies. There are examples involving law firms, unions or impartial individuals agreed by the complainant and the employer. ACAS already plays, as we have seen, an important role in seeking conciliation before tribunal hearings occur, and has a fair success rate. However, in the Employment Rights (Dispute Resolution) Act of 1998, provision was made for ACAS to offer in addition a 'fast track' arbitration scheme for cases involving unfair dismissal only.

---

3   Y. Bennion and A. Rogers, *Courts or Compromise?*, Industrial Society, February 2001.

This scheme took a great deal of time to design, because of concerns about issues raised by the Human Rights Act and over the principle that individuals and employers could not normally appeal against an arbitration decision. It was not launched until the spring of 2001 and came into operation in May of that year in England and Wales (and Scotland later in the year). A great deal of faith was placed in the idea that this form of dispute resolution could reduce the pressure on the tribunal system.

Table 9 describes the main features of the new system, which was broadly welcomed by unions and employers' representatives. As can be seen from the table, the scheme is not simply a cheaper and quicker version of tribunal hearings, and there are some clear departures from tribunal practice. The parties involved agree to forgo the normal tribunal hearing and to rely on the judgment of a member of the ACAS Arbitration Panel, normally comprised of non-lawyers: 60 arbitrators were added to the panel in order to take on the expected expansion in business.

Neither party has a choice of arbitrator in the new scheme. Arbitration is confidential and the results are not made public; it does not set precedents, as it does not make legal judgments; and there is no appeal: both parties must sign a waiver that debars them from going back to a tribunal.

This scheme may appear to offer a useful alternative to the formal tribunal hearing, but it has drawbacks that weaken its attractions. There is no reason to suppose its judgments will be on average any fairer, or less fair, than those of employment tribunals. However, consenting to arbitration is risky for both parties – who both have to agree to the arrangement. Reliance on one person rather than three to make a judgment that cannot be appealed against is likely to deter some applicants and respondents, as is

Table 9 Employment tribunals and ACAS arbitration: a comparison

Unfair dismissal/key process areas	Employment tribunal	Arbitration
Decision (fair or unfair dismissal) is based on	Statute and case law/ 'test of reasonableness'	ACAS Code of Practice and Handbook, general principles of fairness and good conduct
Those hearing the case	Legally qualified chairperson and lay members	ACAS arbitrator with knowledge/experience of employment relations, sitting alone
Location of hearing	ETS office	By agreement at hotel/ ACAS office/workplace/ representatives' premises or other
Length of hearing	Normally at least one day	Normally half a day
Presentation of evidence	Cross-examination of witnesses on oath	Informal presentation, no oaths or cross-examination by parties but questioning by arbitrator
Availability of witnesses and documents	Witness orders, orders for discovery/inspection or production by witnesses of documents	No powers in scheme to make orders, but failure of parties to cooperate can count against them when decision is made
Expenses to attend hearing/ loss of earnings	Tribunal can reimburse expenses and losses for parties, witnesses and some representatives	No expenses paid by ACAS, but compensation for unfair dismissals may include a sum for cost of attending hearing
Remedies/awards	Statutory provisions/ interim relief available	ACAS scheme/interim relief not available
Publicity	Public hearing and award	Private hearing/confidential award
Appeal/challenge	Can be made to EAT and appellate courts	No appeal on point of law or fact (other than EC law or Human Rights Act issues), challenge only for jurisdiction and serious irregularity

Source: From The ACAS arbitration scheme for the resolution of unfair dismissal disputes: a guide to the scheme, ACAS, 2001.

the fact that arbitrators are not bound by legal precedents. One employer, questioned in a survey[4] of attitudes to the new scheme, for instance, observed that 'three nutters were better than one egotist', though this may admittedly be a fine call.

There is also some residual doubt as to whether the lack of appeal procedure can be maintained. Parties can appeal for judicial review of an arbitrator's decision in the Queen's Bench Division, and it is still theoretically possible for an aggrieved applicant to pursue redress through the European Court, where an adverse ruling could undermine the rationale for the scheme.

The fact that the procedure is confidential will certainly appeal to businesses, but probably less so to employees, who may wish for their 'day in court' to justify themselves. Some may also wish to use the threat of publicity as leverage against employers or simply as a form of revenge.[5] There may also be a public-interest issue here; it can be argued that the public has a right to know the outcome of publicly funded arbitration.

Another factor to be borne in mind is that, for high-profile cases, the financially strongest party (which may be a union representing a group of workers rather than an employer) may wish to prolong proceedings in the hope of forcing withdrawal or concessions from the other party.

It is unlikely that the scheme will have a major impact. It applies only to those who are pursuing just an unfair dismissal case (the large number of applications that cover other tribunal jurisdictions as well as unfair dismissal cannot be dealt with in this way). It seems to be assumed that only those cases that ACAS

---

4   See J. Earnshaw and S. Hardy, 'Assessing an Arbitral Route for Unfair Dismissal', *Industrial Law Journal*, 30, 3 September 2001, p. 298.

5   Ibid., p. 303.

currently fails to conciliate or which are not settled by some other means will volunteer for the arbitration route, thus reducing the number coming forward to tribunals. On this basis ACAS speculated that up to 1,000 cases a year might go to arbitration rather than a tribunal hearing. The CBI was more optimistic, suggesting the scheme might handle 5,000 cases a year. This now seems highly unlikely, as in the first six months of operation just five cases were dealt with.[6]

While business may pick up as the scheme becomes more widely known, it does not necessarily follow that the number of unfair dismissal cases going to tribunals will therefore fall. Only a small fraction of cases actually reach a tribunal hearing anyway. It is possible that many of those whose cases would have been conciliated, abandoned or settled by other means might in the future opt for arbitration, thus giving ACAS a sizeable workload (and a further addition to the costs borne by the public) while the numbers going to tribunal hearings continue unchanged.

DTI proposals and the Employment Bill

In the summer of 2001, the DTI published a consultation document[7] containing a series of linked proposals for changes in procedures and requirements, which the department's economists estimated might lead to an overall reduction of tribunal applications of between 16 and 19 per cent per year, offering a saving to

---

6   See J. Eaglesham, 'Employment arbitration scheme fails to take off', *Financial Times*, 11 December 2001.

7   Department of Trade and Industry, *Routes to Resolution: Improving Dispute Resolution in Britain*, July 2001.

employers of between £47 and £63 million in 2000/01 terms. A consultation period of just under twelve weeks produced almost two hundred responses, a summary of which was published by the DTI in November.[8] Following this, most of the proposals were incorporated into the new Employment Bill. A summary of the DTI proposals, some comments, and the DTI response to consultation is given in Table 10.

It was also agreed that an Employment Tribunal System Taskforce (chaired by Janet Gaymer) should be set up to make recommendations on rendering tribunals more efficient and cost effective. This taskforce was due to report in the spring of 2002 but, as previously explained, its findings have not yet been published.

Many of the detailed proposals are rather fiddly suggestions which will have little impact on the overall number of applications or their outcomes – for example, the new requirement for all applications to be made on the official form (at the moment tribunals can use their discretion to accept the small number of other written applications).

Some are more important. In future all employers, however small, will have to provide written details of grievance and disciplinary procedures, which must meet a basic minimum standard.[9] The requirement for all employers to have such procedures is the basis for requiring an employee to exhaust all internal procedures before applying to tribunals. The DTI has estimated that this new requirement could reduce annual applications by

---

8 Department of Trade and Industry, *Routes to Resolution: Government Response*, 8 November 2001.

9 Three-stage disciplinary and grievance procedures must involve written statements, a formal meeting and reporting procedure and provision for appeal.

Table 10 **The DTI proposals**

Proposal	Comment
RESOLVING DISPUTES AT WORK	
Only allowing applications to tribunals once workplace disciplinary or grievance procedures have been completed	DTI expects big fall in applications as more disputes resolved internally. *Agreed and included in Employment Bill.*
Increasing or reducing awards where employer or employee had unreasonably failed to take a set of minimum procedural actions	Formalising and extending existing situation for employer: new pressure on employee. *Agreed and included in Employment Bill. Minimum procedures for grievances to be an implied contractual term.*
Awarding additional compensation to an employee to reflect the absence of a written statement of employment terms	Only small impact expected. *Agreed and included in Employment Bill.*
Removing the current 20-employee threshold for including details of disciplinary or grievance procedures in the written statement	Small impact expected. *Agreed and included in Employment Bill.*
Allowing tribunals to disregard procedural mistakes in unfair dismissal cases if no difference to the outcome	Sensible minor amendment to procedures. *Agreed. Provided minimum standards for internal resolution of disputes are met, Employment Bill to allow minor procedural shortfalls to be ignored.*
PROMOTING CONCILIATION	
Introducing a fixed period for conciliation	Intended to speed resolution. DTI estimates that this will marginally reduce number of tribunal hearings. *Agreed and included in Employment Bill.*
Broadening the scope of compromise agreements to match ACAS-conciliated settlements	This proposal would remove residual right to go to a tribunal after a compromise agreement. *Agreed. Legislation to be amended.*
Enabling other organisations to provide conciliation alongside ACAS	Problematic – standards and public funding issues. *Proposal abandoned.*
MODERNISING TRIBUNALS	
Introducing charging for applications and when a case is listed for hearing	Politically controversial and of limited effect because of likely high level of exemptions. *Proposal abandoned before consultation process completed.*
Including in awards of costs compensation for the time a party spends dealing with claim; changing presumption to award costs against weak cases	Little impact as costs rarely awarded anyway. *Agreed and included in Employment Bill.*
Allowing tribunals to make orders for wasted costs against representatives who charge	A feeling that lawyers inflate costs. This power unlikely to be used much. *Agreed and included in Employment Bill.*
Making standard application form mandatory	Bureaucratic convenience. Arguably might penalise applicants with poor writing skills. *Agreed and included in Employment Bill.*
Enabling Tribunal Presidents (Lord Chancellor in England) to issue guidance on procedure	To facilitate common approaches by different tribunals. *Agreed and included in Employment Bill.*
Introducing a fast track for certain jurisdictions	Cut ACAS out of the loop for, e.g., breach of conduct, redundancy claims. *Agreed.*
Registering applications publicly only when claim has been listed for hearing	Not publishing details early may encourage settlement. *To be considered further.*

20,000 or so, although it will not be costless[10] and will have to be phased in.

Its impact, however, may be significantly less than the government hopes. The requirement for employees to exhaust procedures before applications are accepted will not be absolute; it can be waived 'in case of serious bullying or intimidation'. It seems likely, therefore, that we will witness an upsurge in alleged bullying, something which, outside the physical brutality of closed institutions such as prisons, boarding schools and the armed forces, can be a highly subjective phenomenon. Given the context of many micro-firms, it also seems likely that their formal procedures will be something of a farce. In an owner-managed firm appeals against the decision of the boss will be heard by the boss. This is unlikely to resolve problems. As we saw in the previous chapter, there are in any case doubts that the existence of formal procedures does much in itself to deter tribunal applications. The Better Regulation Task Force has recommended that ACAS should pilot a free or subsidised mediation service[11] for businesses with less than 50 employees, and this is a possible way in which employers might be able to encourage employees in smaller firms to reflect before applying to tribunals.

One suggestion that might have some impact is the proposal to limit publicity of claims until they are listed for hearing. The view here is that publicity before the conciliation phase might increase intransigence and discourage attempts to reach a compromise.

---

10   The DTI estimates that setting up procedures where firms do not already possess them will cost between £46 and £86 million. However, there is an estimated saving in tribunal application costs of £65–90 million.

11   Better Regulation Task Force, *Employment Regulation: striking a balance*, May 2002, p. 28.

Employers might also see this as reducing the pressure on them to pay people off for damaging, albeit unfounded, claims.

The proposals that attracted most attention when published were those which would have introduced charges for applications and hearings and increased penalties for frivolous or vexatious applications. Trade unionists reacted strongly against these proposals and the government soon indicated that it would not pursue them. It appears that charges for applications would produce so many exemptions on the basis of low incomes that the administrative costs would not justify the small reduction in applications that the proposal might produce. Tribunals already possess the power to penalise vexatious applicants, but they have been reluctant to do so, and it is unlikely that any new penalties would have had a significant impact on the level of applications. Although there is some increased power to award costs introduced in the Employment Bill, the DTI economists' estimates suggest that any impact on applications will be negligible.

In general, the DTI proposals that have made it to the Employment Bill seem modest in their aspirations and likely consequences. They do not really address the reasons why tribunal applications have grown and do not challenge the assumptions of the system as it has grown up over recent decades. Furthermore, other elements of the bill, such as those which implement the EU Directive on fixed-term work and introduce an 'equal pay questionnaire' for tribunal cases, may even lead to an increase in tribunal business over time.

Do we need tribunals in their current form?

One issue that has rarely been debated is the composition of employment tribunals. Ever since their inception during the Wilson administration, when tripartite bodies such as the National Economic Development Council were all the rage, it has been taken for granted that these bodies should be drawn from the 'two sides of industry', with a legal chair representing the state. For many years nominations to the list of lay members were in the hands of the unions (through the TUC) and employers' organisations such as the CBI. Unsurprisingly, nomination by such bodies led to considerable under-representation of women, ethnic minorities, and employers and employees drawn from small businesses.

Challenges to the composition of the lay panels, most recently under the Human Rights Act, have led to a reform in procedures which allows individuals to nominate themselves in response to public advertisement, with appointment decisions being much more dependent on objective qualifications. This has led to some changes to the social make-up of panels. The most recent intake of 324 lay members, chosen from almost 9,000 applicants, had 54 per cent female membership, 17 per cent from ethnic minorities, and 18 per cent with experience of working with some form of disability.[12]

However, the range of business experience is still biased towards larger companies and the public sector. Few owners or managers of small businesses, let alone employees within such businesses, can afford the time (members have to be available for at least fifteen days a year) to be panel members. Moreover, those business representatives on the employer panels tend to be drawn from a personnel management background rather than from other areas of the business such as finance, marketing or

---

12　Data provided by the ETS.

information technology. Information on the background of representatives is very limited, but examples of CVs in ETS recruitment packs and other sources suggest that employer representatives are often retired or semi-retired (panel members can go on working until the age of 72) human resource consultants and personnel managers, often with a public sector background.

People from this background are unlikely to be at the cutting edge of today's competitive business world. With a feeling for consensus, and imbued with the conventional wisdom of human resource management gurus, they are likely to be as sympathetic to tribunal applications as are the employee representatives. Those involved with tribunals often proudly point out that the employee and employer representatives rarely split along sectional lines, but seem to reach similar conclusions on cases before them. This is held to be a good thing. However, it can be argued that a representative panel of employers *ought* to see things slightly differently, and recognise that the human resource management framework of ordered, structured workplaces with procedures for every eventuality and good relations with recognised unions is not easily applicable to small entrepreneurial businesses with a younger workforce and different assumptions about the world of employment. Practices and expectations that are feasible in long-established and highly structured workplaces may not be easily transferable to the more fluid environment of start-up businesses.

As we move farther and farther away from the industrial relations environment and assumptions of the 1960s, it is surprising that we still maintain the balanced 'two sides of industry' tribunals of the past. To some extent these arrangements have been shored up by the emphasis on the corporatist rhetoric of 'social partners' which permeates much of the thinking of the European Commission. But awareness of this should not preclude some lateral thinking on the problems of tribunals.

Could we not think of more issues where chairpersons could sit alone without lay members? Could we think of a new breed of trained professional assessors, rather than lawyers backed up by what might unkindly be called amateurs? This would not reduce the number of tribunal applications, but it might make for a faster service and possibly one that could generate a more consistent set of expectations amongst employers.

Other ways of regulating

Thinking farther out of the box, are there not areas of labour market regulation which might be taken away from the realm of individual applications and instead be the prerogative of an inspectorate rather than the tribunal system? We do not rely on individual workers to take up claims of breaches of health and safety regulations, so why should (say) equal pay issues not be dealt with by inspectors? Arguably, because many equal pay issues are nowadays concerned with forms of alleged indirect discrimination against groups of workers rather than individuals, such an approach to enforcement is more appropriate.

An inspectorate might be more expensive, and few employers would initially welcome it, but it might have the advantage of bringing greater certainty into the legal environment. It would also remove the element of malicious or vexatious tribunal application which employers fear. If employees really do need protection, an inspectorate might be more effective in ensuring that the weaker and less articulate members of the workforce get it; at the moment, the tribunal system favours the better educated, at least over some types of claim. As Nick Burkitt[13] has pointed out, most aspects of minimum wage enforcement are dealt with by Inland Revenue inspectors rather than employment tribunals; is this approach capable of wider application in labour market regulation?

Another variant on this is to suggest that, if the function of labour market regulation is primarily to enhance perceived 'fairness', could not greater use be made of the tax and benefit system – monetary adjustments funded by the taxpayer rather than employer mandates, the burden of which is not transparent?

For example, in redressing disadvantages faced by people with disabilities, it is likely to be more efficient to provide grants or specific offsetting payments to individuals rather than to require employers to restructure their business practices and, if they do not do so, force individuals to go through the tribunal system to seek redress. To take another area, if redundancy payments other than those privately agreed are necessary, why should they not be paid by the state rather than the employer? They were at one time.

The Better Regulation Task Force points out that:

> There are always different ways of dealing with a policy objective. For example, to encourage mothers to return to the labour market, the Swedish Government has made childcare very affordable … as low as £65 a month … The Swedish Government has taken the conscious decision to provide heavily subsidised childcare as its main instrument to make the labour market more attractive to mothers, rather than using regulations which impose more of a burden on employers.[14]

---

13   N. Burkitt, 'Workers' wrongs', *Guardian*, 17 August 2001.
14   Better Regulation Task Force, op. cit., p. 14.

The introduction of inspectorates or tax-funded benefits produces its own problems, and the unpopular cost of higher taxation falls on employers and workers. But such approaches have the merit of explicitness. They produce greater certainty for employers – and we have seen that the uncertainty surrounding the legal environment is the cause of speculative applications by employees and inadvertent breaches of the law by employers.

If such changes alert the public to the real costs of labour market interventions, so much the better for policy. One reason why there has been such an enormous growth in labour market intervention is that the public is largely oblivious to the costs of a system where tribunals spend other people's money and labour market regulation imposes what are in effect 'stealth taxes' which reduce employment.

The commissions

We have seen that applications concerning discrimination have been rising faster than many other types of application. Such applications do not, however, have a very high success rate. We noted earlier the role that publicly funded commissions representing particular sections of the workforce – the Equal Opportunities Commission (EOC), the Commission for Racial Equality and the Disability Rights Commission – play in encouraging and supporting tribunal claims.

The danger of the commissions is that they come to be dominated by a particular ideology or approach which is not necessarily typical of the group whose interests they are intended to promote – let alone the wider population – and which may often be based on dubious economic analysis. Their support for tribunal cases may be playing a significant part in the surge of applications under discrimination jurisdictions.

In addition to pursuing and even soliciting tribunal claims, they may become political advocates for particular policies that continually tend to increase government intervention. For example, the EOC's claim that a persistent gap in pay between men and women is almost solely the result of discrimination by intransigent employers ignores much of the evidence about how variations in pay occur in market economies. It leads them to advocate ever greater interference in wage-setting, recruitment and promotion, and currently leads them, for example, to advocate compulsory 'equal pay audits' within companies.

As indicated earlier, European Union directives banning discrimination on grounds of religion or sexual orientation come into force in 2003, while age discrimination becomes illegal in 2006. The European law that requires these new rights directs the government to nominate a body to oversee them. None of the existing commissions seems particularly suited to dealing with these new jurisdictions, but the prospect of creating three new commissions is not one that the government favours.

A proposal mooted some time ago by the Lord Chancellor, and supported by the Federation of Small Businesses, is the merger of the existing commissions to form an over-arching Human Rights Commission which would also embrace the new jurisdictions. This has something in its favour. At the moment, the objectives of the commissions may be in conflict to a significant degree. For example, the EOC's objective of narrowing or eliminating the pay gap between men and women would, taken literally and with no offsetting changes elsewhere, have the effect of increasing inequality between households from different ethnic groups.[15] This is clearly something which would disturb the Commission for Racial Equality, and provoke demands for yet more government intervention.

A Human Rights Commission would have to confront the contradictions in the agendas of particular pressure groups, and this might lead to more sensible policy proposals. Against this, however, is the danger that such a commission would accumulate still wider powers to interfere with labour markets and to present itself, bolstered by its EU credentials, as a challenger to Parliament and the judiciary.

At the moment, the government seems to favour the creation of some sort of single equality body 'in the longer term', and is expected to produce outline proposals in the autumn of 2002. With some reservations, the CBI appears to have signed up to this principle.[16]

The design of this new body is crucial if it is not to turn into an overbearing influence. In particular the government should look seriously at minimising its powers to act as an advocate for further regulation, and not allow it to use public money to promote particular interpretations of labour market outcomes. Its role in relation to tribunal applications should also be more narrowly defined than is currently the case.

---

15 White women, who dominate the female workforce, already earn more than men from a number of ethnic minority groups. See J. R. Shackleton and P. Urwin, 'Men and the Labour Market', in E. Pizzey, J. R. Shackleton and P. Urwin, *Men or Women – Who Are the Victims?*, Civitas, London, 2000.

16 J. Eaglesham, 'Single equality body set to be created', *Financial Times*, 13 May 2002.

A return to voluntarism?

It is difficult to see how any reform measures could significantly reduce the number of tribunal applications without reversing the underlying trend for governments increasingly to interfere with labour markets. Thus a radical agenda would have to embrace substantial deregulation and a much larger role for freedom of contract. Employers and employees would, by and large, be left free to form contracts with each other without the present mass of government-imposed rules. The result would not necessarily be a system in which every individual bargained separately with potential employers with automatic resort to the law when things went wrong. Employees might still choose to bargain in groups, through unions or other organisations, under such a regime, and both employers and employees might well decide to protect themselves against unexpected events through insurance.

At the moment, there does not seem to be much popular support for such an initiative, which might be even harder to implement than were the trade union reforms of the 1980s. At least in that case the unions had made themselves unpopular with large sections of the population, whereas opposition to the extension of individual rights at work remains associated only with a section of employers.

One problem is that opposition to government regulation is understandably often confused with opposition to improving employment conditions. There is a business case for being a 'good' employer, and it is frequently made by worthy organisations such as the Chartered Institute of Personnel and Development, the Work Foundation (formerly the Industrial Society) and the Royal Society for the Arts.

Put simply, the argument is that employers should care about their workers as individuals, treat them fairly, pay them well, be flexible about their working hours, and invest in their training. In return they will gain employee loyalty, enjoy reduced labour turnover and absenteeism, and benefit from higher productivity.[17] Many of our leading companies have built their competitive advantage on this insight. However, it does not follow from this that there is an unequivocal gain to the economy if all employers are forced to meet the standards of the best through the imposition of regulations and mandates.

For one thing, not all employees are seeking the same package of benefits, and a mandatory set of conditions reduces choice: some workers prefer more pay and fewer holidays. Second, firms that are forced to come up to the employment standards of the leaders will fail to get first-mover advantage. Workers will not see their employers as responsible for their improved conditions and will not display any greater loyalty, or higher productivity, than before. Firms will be faced with increased costs without any corresponding benefits.

A further observation is that 'good' employers will often, as part of a strategy of raising rivals' costs, advocate employment mandates in the hope of reducing their rivals' competitiveness – the firm's counterpart of the EOC's argument against 'social dumping'. For what exactly is a 'good' employer? The question is posed in some analysis by Edward Lazear. He remarks that 'taxes or restrictions that affect labour-intensive firms more than they do

---

17   See S. Holtermann, 'The Costs and Benefits to British Employers of Measures to Promote Equality of Opportunity', in J. Humphries and J. Rubery (eds), *The Economics of Equal Opportunity*, Equal Opportunities Commission, 1995; S. Bevan, S. Dench, P. Tomkin and J. Cummings, *Family-Friendly Employment: The Business Case*, Institute for Employment Studies, Research Report 136, 1999.

capital-intensive firms will be favoured by relatively capital-intensive firms. As long as one firm's costs go up by less than the cost of its rivals, it benefits in a competitive environment'.[18]

Lazear discusses the US Coal Mine Health and Safety Act, which became law in the 1970s. It required the installation of safety equipment that was much more costly for eastern mines, which were primarily small-scale and underground, than for western mines, which were primarily large-scale strip mines. Unsurprisingly the legislation was opposed by mining companies in the eastern states – but it was supported by companies in the western states that stood to gain a cost advantage over their rivals. Did that make western mine-owners 'good' employers, or merely opportunistic ones?

Much regulation reduces the ways in which firms can compete. It reduces incentives to innovation, entrenches the market dominance of existing firms, and ultimately tends to slow economic growth. This is a hard idea to get over to the general public, which concentrates on the visible benefits to a sector of the workforce, such as parents or disabled people or older workers advantaged by a new proposal, while not being fully aware of the less overt costs. These costs, as indicated earlier, often fall on people who are unaware of the causes of their difficulties in finding jobs, or keeping them in economic downturns.

Excessive regulation of labour market conditions means that artificially imposed employment standards cannot be indefinitely maintained. The former German Democratic Republic (GDR) provides a salutary lesson. In the GDR, workers enjoyed excellent training, holiday camps, free medical care, workplace nurseries and

---

18   E. P. Lazear, *Personnel Economics*, MIT Press, Cambridge, Mass., 1996, p. 116.

universal pensions – all paid for by the employer. Many UK trade unionists used to hold the East German system up as something to be emulated here. However, the downside was that the system also involved limited job mobility and rigid pay structures. Innovation was stifled, personal freedom was restricted and productivity was abysmal: many enterprises contributed negative value-added to the economy. The system ultimately collapsed when opened up to the rest of the world after the fall of the Berlin Wall.[19] More than a decade later, workers in eastern Germany continue to suffer high levels of unemployment and insecurity.

Historically, widespread and enduring increases in employees' pay and improvements in other conditions of service have not come through government intervention. They have been the result of economic growth, with increased investment in capital equipment, research and development, education and skills on the part of firms and individuals.

Such year-on-year improvements in living standards, evident to any analyst of labour markets with a historical bent, contrast with the increasing use of tribunals, which seems to suggest that employment conditions are getting worse, or are increasingly intolerable. Improvements in working conditions and the continued generation of new job opportunities are more likely to continue if we place more emphasis on allowing employers to reach voluntary agreements with their employees and less on telling them exactly how to do so.

Turning back the tide of recent regulatory developments will be very difficult. Because of the important influence of EU

---

19   J. R. Shackleton and T. Lange, 'The Labour Market in Eastern Germany', in J. R. Shackleton and T. Lange (eds), *The Political Economy of German Unification*, Berghahn Books, Oxford, 1998.

initiatives, it is no longer sufficient to offer policy advice to UK legislators; rather one must address a common agenda throughout the EU. While increasing numbers of economists across Europe are becoming aware of the extent to which regulation is contributing to poor labour market performance, this awareness has yet to penetrate politicians' thinking to the extent necessary for any comprehensive reform.

8   CONCLUSIONS

In this Hobart Paper we have traced the growth of applications to employment tribunals and in the range of subjects now covered by these institutions, which did not exist until the mid-1960s. The decline of trade unionism since the 1970s has seen a movement away from 'collective' to 'individual' rights, enforced through the tribunal system. This trend has been accentuated by changes in the composition of the workforce. There are more women and ethnic minorities employed today than ever before, and labour market regulation has increasingly reflected what policy-makers perceive to be the interests of these groups.

The tribunal system has grown piecemeal to a size where it now imposes significant costs on the economy as a whole – in terms of uncertainty, tension and stress at work, erosion of trust, addition to business costs and, most importantly, discouragement of job creation.

The labour market regulation that tribunals enforce is a form of 'stealth taxation' on employment which impacts on the economy as a whole. Despite widespread belief to the contrary, it is not just employers who bear the cost; workers pay in terms of lower wages and reduced job opportunities.

This burden falls unequally on different groups of employees and potential employees. Moreover, analysis of applications suggests that some types of individual are better placed than others to access the tribunal system, and that this way of enforcing labour market rules would not be particularly well targeted even if these rules were considered desirable. It also suggests, surprisingly, that large firms, the public sector and voluntary bodies are disproportionately likely to face discrimination claims, despite these types of organisations devoting considerable resources to promoting equal opportunities.

The government is currently promoting some procedural changes in an effort to reduce the incidence of tribunal applications, and has set up a taskforce to seek other improvements. The planned changes, however, seem unlikely to alter the picture dramatically. A more radical procedural change would be to accept that the notion of a tribunal with representatives from 'both sides of industry' is a 1960s leftover which is as out of date as kaftans and love beads and which should be replaced by a more streamlined system. Another partial answer to the explosion of tribunal claims may be to alter the form of regulation, with different means of enforcement.

There is also a case for reducing the powers and influence of the commissions that promote potentially contradictory anti-discrimination policies in pursuing the interests of their client groups. The government's current inclination to merge these bodies offers an opportunity for further reform, perhaps confining them to a more narrow informational role than their current position as advocates.

But none of these measures is likely to have much impact on the numbers applying to tribunals so long as the seemingly inexhaustible drive for further labour market regulation from the EU continues to keep employers' and employees' expectations in flux. The way in which EU measures are incorporated in the UK is not helped by loosely drafted legislation, ad hoc changes in interpretation and the current government's unwillingness to antagonise interest groups. New jurisdictions such as age discrimination promise further instability and uncertainty in the future. There is, therefore, potential for the number of tribunal cases to increase still further. As we have seen, they are comparatively limited compared with countries such as Germany.

The only way fundamentally to stem the growth of tribunal applications is therefore to call a halt to further regulation, and instead to begin to move towards greater freedom of contract in labour markets. At the moment there is not much enthusiasm for this in the UK, perhaps because the current relatively low level of unemployment (partly the result of a broadly sound macroeconomic regime in recent years) mutes criticism of regulation initiatives. There is even less enthusiasm in the other EU countries for reform, at least within mainstream political parties whose politicians are afraid to confront their electorates with a clear analysis of the choices open to them.

Things can change, however. If the European economies fall into a recession, this may remind people forcefully that employers who create jobs are more likely to be public benefactors in the long run than those who seek to restrict ever more narrowly the conditions under which employment contracts can be formed.

ABOUT THE IEA

The Institute is a research and educational charity (No. CC 235 351), limited by guarantee. Its mission is to improve understanding of the fundamental institutions of a free society with particular reference to the role of markets in solving economic and social problems.

The IEA achieves its mission by:

- a high-quality publishing programme
- conferences, seminars, lectures and other events
- outreach to school and college students
- brokering media introductions and appearances

The IEA, which was established in 1955 by the late Sir Antony Fisher, is an educational charity, not a political organisation. It is independent of any political party or group and does not carry on activities intended to affect support for any political party or candidate in any election or referendum, or at any other time. It is financed by sales of publications, conference fees and voluntary donations.

In addition to its main series of publications the IEA also publishes a quarterly journal, *Economic Affairs*, and has two specialist programmes – Environment and Technology, and Education.

The IEA is aided in its work by a distinguished international Academic Advisory Council and an eminent panel of Honorary Fellows. Together with other academics, they review prospective IEA publications, their comments being passed on anonymously to authors. All IEA papers are therefore subject to the same rigorous independent refereeing process as used by leading academic journals.

IEA publications enjoy widespread classroom use and course adoptions in schools and universities. They are also sold throughout the world and often translated/reprinted.

Since 1974 the IEA has helped to create a world-wide network of 100 similar institutions in over 70 countries. They are all independent but share the IEA's mission.

Views expressed in the IEA's publications are those of the authors, not those of the Institute (which has no corporate view), its Managing Trustees, Academic Advisory Council members or senior staff.

Members of the Institute's Academic Advisory Council, Honorary Fellows, Trustees and Staff are listed on the following page.

The Institute gratefully acknowledges financial support for its publications programme and other work from a generous benefaction by the late Alec and Beryl Warren.

Other papers recently published by the IEA include:

WHO, What and Why?

Transnational Government, Legitimacy and the World Health Organization
Roger Scruton
Occasional Paper 113; ISBN 0 255 36487 3
£8.00

The World Turned Rightside Up

A New Trading Agenda for the Age of Globalisation
John C. Hulsman
Occasional Paper 114; ISBN 0 255 36495 4
£8.00

The Representation of Business in English Literature

Introduced and edited by Arthur Pollard
Readings 53; ISBN 0 255 36491 1
£12.00

Anti-Liberalism 2000

The Rise of New Millennium Collectivism
David Henderson
Occasional Paper 115; ISBN 0 255 36497 0
£7.50

Capitalism, Morality and Markets

Brian Griffiths, Robert A. Sirico, Norman Barry & Frank Field

Readings 54; ISBN 0 255 36496 2

£7.50

A Conversation with Harris and Seldon

Ralph Harris & Arthur Seldon

Occasional Paper 116; ISBN 0 255 36498 9

£7.50

Malaria and the DDT Story

Richard Tren & Roger Bate

Occasional Paper 117; ISBN 0 255 36499 7

£10.00

A Plea to Economists Who Favour Liberty: Assist the Everyman

Daniel B. Klein

Occasional Paper 118; ISBN 0 255 36501 2

£10.00

Waging the War of Ideas

John Blundell

Occasional Paper 119; ISBN 0 255 36500 4

£10.00

The Changing Fortunes of Economic Liberalism

Yesterday, Today and Tomorrow
David Henderson
Occasional Paper 105 (new edition); ISBN 0 255 36520 9
£12.50

The Global Education Industry

Lessons from Private Education in Developing Countries
James Tooley
Hobart Paper 141 (new edition); ISBN 0 255 36503 9
£12.50

Saving Our Streams

*The Role of the Anglers' Conservation Association in
Protecting English and Welsh Rivers*
Roger Bate
Research Monograph 53; ISBN 0 255 36494 6
£10.00

Better Off Out?

The Benefits or Costs of EU Membership
Brian Hindley & Martin Howe
Occasional Paper 99 (new edition); ISBN 0 255 36502 0
£10.00

Buckingham at 25

Freeing the Universities from State Control
Edited by James Tooley
Readings 55; ISBN 0 255 36512 8
£15.00

Lectures on Regulatory and Competition Policy

Irwin M. Stelzer
Occasional Paper 120; ISBN 0 255 36511 X
£12.50

Misguided Virtue

False Notions of Corporate Social Responsibility
David Henderson
Hobart Paper 142; ISBN 0 255 36510 1
£12.50

HIV and Aids in Schools

The Political Economy of Pressure Groups and Miseducation
Barrie Craven, Pauline Dixon, Gordon Stewart & James Tooley
Occasional Paper 121; ISBN 0 255 36522 5
£10.00

The Road to Serfdom

The Reader's Digest *condensed version*
Friedrich A. Hayek
Occasional Paper 122; ISBN 0 255 36530 6
£7.50

Bastiat's *The Law*

Introduction by Norman Barry
Occasional Paper 123; ISBN 0 255 36509 8
£7.50

A Globalist Manifesto for Public Policy

Charles Calomiris
Occasional Paper 124; ISBN 0 255 36525 X
£7.50

Euthanasia for Death Duties

Putting Inheritance Tax Out of Its Misery
Barry Bracewell-Milnes
Research Monograph 54; ISBN 0 255 36513 6
£10.00

Liberating the Land

The Case for Private Land-use Planning
Mark Pennington
Hobart Paper 143; ISBN 0 255 36508 x
£10.00

IEA Yearbook of Government Performance 2002/2003

Edited by Peter Warburton
Yearbook 1; ISBN 0 255 36532 2
£15.00

Britain's Relative Economic Performance, 1870–1999

Nicholas Crafts
Research Monograph 55; ISBN 0 255 36524 1
£10.00

Should We Have Faith in Central Banks?

Otmar Issing
Occasional Paper 125; ISBN 0 255 36528 4
£7.50

The Dilemma of Democracy

Arthur Seldon

Hobart Paper 136 (reissue); ISBN 0 255 36536 5

£10.00

Capital Controls: a 'Cure' Worse Than the Problem?

Forrest Capie

Research Monograph 56; ISBN 0 255 36506 3

£10.00

The Poverty of 'Development Economics'

Deepak Lal

Hobart Paper 144 (reissue); ISBN 0 255 36519 5

£15.00

Should Britain Join the Euro?

The Chancellor's Five Tests Examined

Patrick Minford

Occasional Paper 126; ISBN 0 255 36527 6

£7.50

Post-Communist Transition: Some Lessons

Leszek Balcerowicz

Occasional Paper 127; ISBN 0 255 36533 0

£7.50

A Tribute to Peter Bauer

John Blundell et al.

Occasional Paper 128; ISBN 0 255 36531 4

£10.00

To order copies of currently available IEA papers, or to enquire about availability, please write (no postage required from within the UK) to:

Lavis Marketing
IEA orders
FREEPOST LON21280
Oxford OX3 7BR

Or contact Lavis Marketing on:
Tel: 01865 767575
Fax: 01865 750079
Email: orders@lavismarketing.co.uk

The IEA also offers a subscription service to its publications. For a single annual payment, currently £40.00 in the UK, you will receive every title the IEA publishes across the course of a year, invitations to events, and discounts on our extensive back catalogue. For more information, please contact:

Subscriptions
The Institute of Economic Affairs
2 Lord North Street
London SW1P 3LB

Tel: 020 7799 8900
Fax: 020 7799 2137
Website: www.iea.org.uk